To my trans sisters

'Overflowing with hard-won wisdom and compassionate insight, Charlie Craggs' *To My Trans Sisters* is a love letter to our community from the women who understand, better than anyone, what our world is like. An invaluable resource for any trans person – and those that love us.'

— *Jennifer Finney Boylan, author of* She's Not There *and* Long Black Veil

'This inspiring collection of letters is essential reading for anyone thinking about transitioning and feels alone, or who wants to understand the diverse experiences trans women have. The messages of hope, humour and triumph over adversity make this book a powerful tool, regardless of where the reader is on the gender spectrum.'

— *Sarah Savage, co-founder of the Trans Pride Brighton charity and co-author of* Are You a Boy or Are You a Girl?

TO MY TRANS SISTERS

TO MY
TRANS SISTERS

Edited by
Charlie Craggs

Jessica Kingsley *Publishers*
London and Philadelphia

First published in 2018
by Jessica Kingsley Publishers
73 Collier Street
London N1 9BE, UK
and
400 Market Street, Suite 400
Philadelphia, PA 19106, USA

www.jkp.com

Copyright © Jessica Kingsley Publishers 2018

Library of Congress Cataloging in Publication Data
A CIP catalog record for this book is available from
the Library of Congress

British Library Cataloguing in Publication Data
A CIP catalogue record for this book is available
from the British Library

ISBN 978 1 78592 343 2
eISBN 978 1 78450 668 1

Printed and bound in the United States

....

This book is dedicated to my best friend Khadija Saye and her mother, my second mum, Mary Mendy, who both lost their lives in the Grenfell Tower fire and who were both instrumental in my transition and in me becoming the woman I am today. I love you both, forever.

....

Contents

Introduction

I created this book because I really struggled in the early days of my transition – I didn't know any other trans girls at the time, so I didn't have a big sister figure in my life to do what a big sister is supposed to do: help me with my make-up, give me dating advice, teach me how be a strong woman. If you're reading this book, there's a good chance you're in that same situation right now. I created this book for you – the book I wish I'd had at the start of my transition. This book will act as that source of sisterly advice, but you don't get just one sister – you get almost 100 and some amazing sisters at that!

From dealing with that 5 o'clock shadow to dealing with transphobia, in sharing the lessons we have learned on our journeys to womanhood, I hope you'll be able to avoid making the same mistakes as us, or at least be prepared for the situations when they occur. After all, sometimes you have to make the mistake yourself to learn the lesson, but at least you can take solace in this book, seeing that we have all been where you are. We made it to the other side, and if we can, you can too, sis.

The women in this book have not only made it *through* transition though, they've made it to the top, and I hope that you can draw inspiration, not only from the advice they share in their letters, but also from the biographies that accompany their letters, detailing what these incredible women have achieved in their lives and careers.

This book contains letters from almost 100 trailblazing trans women: politicians, scientists, models, athletes, authors, actresses, business women, activists, musicians, veterans, beauty queens, religious leaders, celebrities and straight-up trans icons; women of all different ages, races, creeds and sexualities. Women with different views, different stories and different advice – capturing the diversity of the trans experience.

But as different as the women and their stories are, there is one common thing that runs through each letter and the veins of each woman featured in this book: resilience. We are some strong ass women. Almost every letter in this book contains stories of prejudice, rejection, hate – but despite all the hardship girls like us face, we still choose to exist, bravely, boldly and beautifully. It is an achievement to simply survive in this world as a trans woman, but as the women in this book show, not only do we survive, we thrive.

This book is here to support you at the start of your journey, but I urge you to go out and find your sisters in real life too. They will get you through the tough times, because only our sisters understand the struggle we go through, and will also be there to celebrate you as you take strides forward on this journey to becoming who you truly are. In the meantime though, until you find your people, you have this book – we are your people, we are your sisters, we love you.

This book celebrates the women who blazed a trail and created a path for the next generation. This book celebrates you, the next generation of girls at the beginning of your journey. This book celebrates trans sisterhood, in all its excellence.

This book is dedicated *to my trans sisters*... From your trans sisters.

Disclaimer

Transitioning is an intensely personal experience and individual to those who go through it. As a result, the language used by the writers of these letters is specific to their context and how they view themselves and their transition.

Christine Burns

....

Christine Burns, MBE, is a British political activist who was a leading figure in Press for Change (a lobbying and legal support organisation for trans people in the UK formed in 1992). Christine played a pivotal role, alongside colleagues, in obtaining legal recognition for trans people in the UK, working closely with ministers and civil servants during the creation of the Gender Recognition Bill. She was awarded an MBE in 2005 in recognition of her work for trans rights. She was featured on the *Independent on Sunday*'s 2011 Pink List of influential LGBT people in the UK.

....

To my trans sisters,

So you've taken the plunge and begun your transition. Congratulations!

I can imagine that, just in order to get to this landmark moment, you will probably have spent years and years of solitary introspection. You'll have been through every aspect of this in your mind. You'll have drained the Internet dry looking for answers and role models. You'll have tried to work out where these powerful and insistent feelings came from. You'll have looked for ways to make them go away or even just mitigate them. You may have checked out whether you were 'just' a cisgender gay or lesbian, or whether cross-dressing occasionally was the answer. When you exhausted these lines of thought you'll have gone on to agonise over the possible ramifications of permanent transition: Is this going to be the step that ends important relationships forever? Will people – parents, siblings, relatives, friends, co-workers – accept you? Will there be hazards and barriers on the road ahead? Will your GP be a help or a hindrance? Do you want hormones? If so, what problems might you face getting them? Do you feel that surgeries are part of the solution you need? Are you binary or non-binary? Will your post-transition self identify as straight or gay or bisexual? How will potential lovers react to you? Will you be able to keep your job?

I'm not going to try to answer ANY of those questions. Everyone is unique. The right answers for you are what you'll have thought about endlessly already. I won't insult you by assuming you haven't thought hard about every aspect. And I certainly won't presume to offer advice on any of those things. Everyone needs to find the answers that are right for them alone. Besides, the options have changed beyond recognition in the decades since I was in your shoes.

So, what wisdom CAN I offer?

The first thing is that people can surprise you. The people you anticipate being the most likely to reject you may turn out to be unexpected allies. I thought, for instance, that my parents might very possibly reject me. I based that on things they had done and said before they had any inkling of what I was feeling inside, and I delayed my transition for some time because I wasn't sure whether I was ready to cope with losing them. In the event, they turned out to be my staunchest allies and cheerleaders.

We became far closer. I had been so, so, wrong. And the lesson was that we should keep an open mind. I wanted folks to be open-minded about me, but I hadn't kept my mind open about them. It cost me years of needless worry.

The second thing is to be prepared for your viewpoint to change with time and experience. It's inevitable really: you're going to be looking at the world from a completely different vantage point. People will respond to you in new ways, because people DO respond to men and women differently. It stands to reason that your responses will change too. You might think you know who you'll be attracted to, for instance. But our perspectives can change when we have a different body with which to experience intimacy. I'm making no predictions here. Just keep an open mind and heart.

Finally, my advice is to not rush into trans advocacy until you've given yourself time to learn about the very diverse community you're joining. That may sound like an ancient croc of an activist telling the newcomers to watch their place, but it's really not meant from that perspective. It's hugely tempting to want to go out and join the fight. And yet we've all seen people who transition and then – driven by the enthusiasm to communicate and explain – get into hot water because their ideas were still a work in progress. Give it time. Observe what others do and say. The fight will still be there next year. Spend that time reading whatever you can find out about our community's history. That knowledge will make you a better advocate anyway. And compare what you *would* have said in a given debate with what more experienced people are saying. They might not necessarily be right, but asking questions will aid in understanding why we argue one way rather than another.

Anyway, I hope that's helpful. But above all, enjoy the most amazing journey of discovery that any human could go on. The vast majority of the human race will never get the chance to learn what you'll learn in the course of your life ahead. Odd as it may sound, think of that as a privilege.

Lots of love,

Christine Burns, MBE

Laura Jane Grace

....

Laura Jane Grace is the lead singer and guitarist of the popular punk rock band Against Me! Laura came out publicly as trans in May 2012, discussing her gender identity in an interview with *Rolling Stone* magazine, and went on to release 'Transgender Dysphoria Blues', the band's sixth studio album which became their biggest chart success, debuting at No. 23 on the Billboard 200 and at No. 6 on Billboard's Top Rock Albums chart. *TIME* magazine ranked it the 7th best album of 2014, and that same year Laura was included on *The Advocate's* '40 under 40' list. Laura has told her story and discussed her transition in her Emmy-nominated documentary series *True Trans* and in her memoir, *Tranny: Confessions of Punk Rock's Most Infamous Anarchist Sellout.*

....

To my trans sisters,

This is what I wish someone would have said to me at the very start of my transition...

Whatever vision of self you have in your head, of who the end result is that you're transitioning to, abandon it. That won't be who you become. You have no idea where you're heading and that's okay.

You're under no obligation to transition any certain way, no obligation to stick to your own plan even. There is no hormone or surgical procedure or clothes you can put on your body that make you more or less trans.

At the same time, fuck what anyone else thinks, and if you do want hormones or surgical procedures, or fancy, fabulous, awesome clothes, never feel wrong for it. Live as fully as you can, always without apology.

Trans is power. If people spew hate and discrimination towards you it is because they fear you and they fear you because you are stronger than them, more badass and awesome. The world is full of weak, small-minded people, and that will never change. Don't let them diminish your shine.

There will be days ahead far more dark than you could have ever imagined possible, days full of self-doubt and self-hate when it feels like you've ruined your life and your friendships and family. This may be true. You may lose all your friends and your family may never talk to you again. It's their loss, not yours.

Slow down, be present in the moment. Now is here. Here is now. Focus on all that you do have for certain and appreciate it. Release your grip and accept that you are not in control, that everything and everyone may be gone from your life at any moment, always. In order to change, accept change, and once you have learned how to flow with it, never stop flowing.

There will be days when you want to die. Don't die. Find the edge and walk it, learn to balance on it, you will eventually be able to run along it, do backflips and handstands and laugh wildly in the face of it. Death will always be there waiting; in the meantime, you've got nothing to lose, so live.

Through destruction comes rebirth and in rebirth there is the chance to begin again new. Now is your chance, the chance you've spent all these years dreaming of. Love yourself. I know that's been hard to do for so long, but it's okay, you can do it.

Most importantly, if you ever need a friend, I'm here for you.

Laura Jane Grace

Kate Stone

....

Scientist Kate Stone studied for her PhD in physics and micro-electronics at the University of Cambridge, which led to the creation of her groundbreaking company Novalia. She was invited to give a TED Talk at TED's main annual event in the USA alongside some of the world's greatest minds, about her work, which has been watched almost 700,000 times online. Kate was the first trans person to ever present on the TED stage. In 2014, after being exploited by the British press, she used her bad experience as a catalyst for creating change in the way the media talks about trans people, and now sits on the Editors' Code of Practice Committee.

....

To my trans sisters,

Don't get lost in transition! The aim of transition is to come out the other side. For too many of us transition itself can become the focus. My aim was to achieve obscurity, but I did not know this at the time. However, in the beginning, having spent a lifetime lacking the bravery to shed my outer shell and let my inner self shine, I was so excited about having begun my journey that I felt the need to tell everyone! Anyone – friends, family, strangers, those who would listen and also those who would not. With this less than thoughtful strategy I managed to alienate myself from anyone who knew me and those who had the misfortune of coming into contact with me! My obsession with transition was a journey towards becoming lost in transition, by staring at transition rather than who I would be on the other side.

Once I had driven everyone away and with no one really left to tell, all I could do was focus on being myself. I had a hard time 'passing', and I did not help myself – I wore the highest heels, the shortest skirts and the brightest lipstick, I thought this would help me blend in and feel awesome! Obviously I stuck out like a sore thumb, or as I cruelly used to say to myself 'ram dressed as lamb'.

For the first two years, every day I left my house, I would receive abuse in the street. People would shout at me, stare at me and occasionally throw food at me from their vehicles. I lived on my own, worked on my own and decided to go out on my own. I needed to learn to become my own best friend. I started to realise that what I had spent a lifetime thinking was my greatest weakness was in fact my greatest strength. That strength was me and who I am. I used to hate myself and one day I discovered that I could look myself in the mirror and say, 'I love you', because although I did not like what I saw, I began to learn to like who I saw: a person brave enough to be themselves no matter what anyone else might throw at them. I had begun to discover my superpower. A superpower that could potentially equip me to travel the world, spread kindness and overcome evil.

Although I was initially too scared to go out to any bars and socialize, I eventually decided that I would rather die living than live dying. To sit at home and feel sorry for myself felt like a shortcut to the grave! So I started to go out and sit in the largest bar in the middle of my town, Cambridge. People can be cruel, very cruel, but I was beginning to learn to be kind to myself. I knew I was being stared at, laughed at and pointed at. At times people would even take ice from their drinks and throw it at the back of my head just so they could see my face and laugh as I turned around. On a few occasions things became more violent – at least twice I have being dragged by my arms and legs from a bar for using the bathroom, and on one occasion spent the night in a police cell.

The most difficult thing was not going out and putting up with abuse; the greatest challenge was not allowing myself to get angry and to try to turn my inner bigotry into kindness and understanding towards others. I had never met people like this before and my behaviour towards them was often inappropriate. They had never met anyone like me before and I reciprocated with similar behaviour. As I walked down the street and people stared, I could only imagine what they were thinking about me – none of it was pleasant. But to assume that everyone was thinking the same thing, without knowing them or who they were, actually made me the bigot. One day I decided that as I did not really know what they were thinking, I could in fact choose to make up anything I wanted! So I decided to think that they were looking at me thinking, 'Wow, she is so beautiful' or 'Is she that famous actress?' or 'I wish I could be as brave and confident as her.' Try it, it's lots of fun! I don't believe there is any one fixed version of reality, so we can be free to create our own reality or warp it a little as we wish!

I showed kindness towards even the worst nightclub I had visited, a place that had dragged me to the doors by my arms and legs, thrown me on the street, watched me get beaten up and called the police to have me arrested. After I complained to the owners, they asked me if I would help them and be a part of their diversity training. I was invited to meet the whole security team and tell them about my life. Fifteen members of security sat before me. I told them about my children, that I am a scientist with my own business and that when I go out for a drink I get abuse from strangers. They were horrified and from that day made it their mission to protect me rather than persecute me. This was a huge lesson for me. My own bigotry towards those who hurt me was a part of the problem. I also began to learn the power of storytelling; how to set the scene and use empathy to help move people's perspective – this was a powerful lesson!

After a while, and by learning to smile rather than hide my face, people started to be kind to me and ask me to join their group of friends. Next would come invites to go out to a nightclub and then sometimes a party. The more I focused on being kind to myself and to anyone I encountered, the less I started to think about concepts of passing or blending in. Then one day I realised I did not remember the last time someone had been cruel to me. I had learnt that when I sensed someone staring at me my reaction should be to look up and smile. When they smile back, it gives me goose bumps!

What I discovered was that the goal was not to try to be like everyone else; it was to be like me. The goal was not to shed one layer and then just focus on issues with the new outer layer; it was to go beyond layers. What we look like and where we are from is irrelevant when compared to who we are. We need to let our inner souls shine so brightly that no one can see what we look like. Maybe it's like looking at the sun, so bright that all you can sense is its warmth. I realised that people felt the warmth of my personality and no longer actually saw what I looked like and found it difficult to label me.

I tend to be the sort of person who jumps off into the deep end rather than makes a plan. The way I originally 'came out' in the industry I work in was just the same. At the time, my business was small – just me in fact. I had been invited to speak at an industry event in Germany. I was early in transition and had not actually told anyone I worked with about this. At that time I used to travel to places overseas as 'Kate', arrive, then get changed back into my disguise as my old self. Except this time when I arrived in Frankfurt at the hotel there was a drinks reception for the speakers and I thought, 'What if I discreetly attend as Kate and don't tell anyone!' I also thought that if the people who invited me to speak realised, they would probably be offended and send me home immediately for discrediting them and their event. I slipped into the drinks reception, I turned around directly into my old boss, and he did not recognise me! But the organisers did. I apologised. I was so embarrassed and explained that if they wanted to send me home I would understand. But they said to me that what would be strange was not continuing as I had started – they wanted me to be Kate for the whole event. I was shocked and terrified! I was going to have to go on stage and give a technology talk as my true self. I was not a good speaker – it always terrified me. Well, now I had something else to worry about. My thoughts were that I would never be able to give a talk again. I imagined no one would be able to take me seriously and would just be questioning 'Is that a guy or a girl?' I resigned myself to thinking this would be the last time I could go on a stage and share my work.

I've shared this part of my story because it was the background for one of the most amazing things to happen to me. I continued as Kate in my workplace, and went from strength to strength. I made many contacts through people I met at work, and somehow my passion for what I do and my vision shone even brighter. I was asked to do more and more talks. I discovered that the secret to giving a great talk is to share a story so passionately that any concerns you may have about how you come across or how you look do not get in the way of effective communication. This journey led me to speak to over a thousand people at an event in Switzerland. Someone in the audience from Microsoft was so impressed that he told the people at TED. I met them and they invited me to speak at the TED main annual event in the USA! Never did the subject of being trans come up; it was not a thing. The only advice they gave me was to go on stage, be myself and share the story of what I do in my area of creativity! I later learned that I was the first trans person to present on the TED stage and my story was not about being trans. The message I wanted to convey is being trans is not a 'thing'. The best way I could say this was to not talk about it. To this day I cannot believe that I went from being terrified to giving a talk on a stage amongst the world's greatest minds to an audience of 1800 of the most connected, privileged and powerful people in our society!

I had reached my goal, to be in a place where being trans was a very obscure part of who I was. I no longer considered myself as trans. I'm proud to be trans, and so happy I am, but it does not define me.

In this happy state of reaching trans obscurity I was walking through the woods one night with my friends, perhaps a little drunk, and then my life changed again. Out of the darkness a startled stag (deer) ran into me at high speed, and gored me through the throat with its antler. I was miraculously rescued, airlifted to hospital, had my throat reconstructed and was put into a coma (this is a whole other story – I've kept it short!). The British press made me a into a very disrespectful headline on New Year's Day as I lay in a coma, with family and friends not knowing if I would survive or what kind of recovery I might have.

The worst headline read: 'Sex Swap Scientist Gored by Stag'. They stole my obscurity, and I've honestly never recovered that.

In short, I channelled my anger and disappointment in them into kindness and understanding. Through searching online I found someone who shared my understanding of taking a kind approach. She helped me figure out how to work with them. I helped them realise that what they did was unkind, against their own rules and just plain wrong. My goal was simply to reduce the chances of them doing this to anyone else by using their own complaints system, no matter how imperfect, and by sacrificing my further privacy to realise this goal. It worked, and they worked with me, I was given the opportunity to speak to millions of people through television and radio, and where possible I tried to spread a message of kindness. I did not do this alone – there were some awesome people who worked magic behind the scenes. Six months later I was encouraged to apply to join the committee run by the press that writes their rules. I did and was accepted. I now sit on a panel a few times a year amongst some of the most powerful editors in the UK and have become part of the process that regulates the press. Sitting on that committee (the Editors' Code of Practice Committee) I often exchange niceties over a cup of tea with its Chairman, *Daily Mail* Editor Paul Dacre. I am treated with kindness and respect, listened to and asked for my opinion. I realise that the most important thing I have to do is show up, be present and take my seat at the table. People who work for the newspaper that wrote the worst headline about me I now consider friends of mine. On a few occasions I've spent the day in the Editor's office, and all we talk about is how my work in technology could become a part of what they do. It's just bonkers to think that the person they wrote about is now someone they want to work with to help a struggling industry. I love the irony!

I'm lucky that I managed to subdue my bigotry towards journalists, especially tabloid journalists, and now enjoy their company and conversation.

There have been some cruel moments on my journey, as there have been for many others too. I imagine this story of cruelty is common. However, I discovered the power of kindness and started to realise that I could control the story, that indeed my greatest strength was actually being myself. With each and every cruel moment my strength grew. Those moments gave me the opportunity to bring about change and help society on its transition towards being more accepting of others. This journey for me has been as much about convergence as transition – as I have changed, so has society. The bar that had me arrested had no trans policy until they met me. I didn't realise, but at the time the company owned over half of the nightclubs in the UK. Small acts of kindness can be the seeds of big moments of change. My scary encounter at a conference led me to the TED stage, and a goring by a stag and trampling by the press have given me a seat at the table and a voice.

Sometimes we have to ask ourselves: 'Do I define my day by what happened to me or by what I did in response?'

I feel extremely lucky to be me, to be trans and for each and every thing that has happened to me. Don't become lost in transition. We are extremely lucky to be so special and to have experiences that provide us with insights into humanity, to see life from more than one side and to have an opportunity to develop a personality that can be empathetic and transcend bigotry. Our role, like everyone else's in this world, is to be the most awesome version of ourselves. Shine brightly, sister, spread smiles and the warmth of kindness!

Kate Stone

Isis King

....

Isis King was the first-ever transgender contestant to star on the popular TV show *America's Next Top Model* in 2008, making her one of the most visible transgender people in the world at the time. In 2011 she was invited back to compete on the show's 'All-Stars' series. After her groundbreaking first appearance on the show, she went on to front an American Apparel campaign as their first trans model, had a guest star role in *The Bold and the Beautiful* and was featured on *Candy* magazine's iconic 2015 cover with other trans icons like Laverne Cox, Janet Mock and Carmen Carrera. Isis also recently starred in the hit TV show *Strut*, a GLAAD Award-winning reality series executive produced by Whoopi Goldberg, which follows the lives and careers of five trans models.

....

To my trans sisters,

What do I wish I knew when I began transitioning? It's quite simple actually. I wish I knew that the journey of finding myself would be the journey of a lifetime. When we start our transition, we have a timeline of days and the amount of time it will take to complete the steps to become our true self. Truth is, the journey never ends, the obstacles continue and you learn something new with each passing day, week and year. Enjoy the ride. It will be bumpy, but so worth it when you get to that place of complete comfort in yourself. Transitioning starts your body clock over: you're a baby learning to maneuver your way through life and no one can stop you. One thing that took me a while to learn, which I wish I'd learned earlier, was not looking for external validation – it's inside you. No man, woman, friend, parent, boyfriend or girlfriend can fill that thing inside of you. That's your journey. Feel fulfilled within first, be comfortable in your own skin. Only then will you become that positive light that you are meant to be in this wicked world.

It's inside of you.

Blessings,

Isis

Kim Coco Iwamoto

....

Kim Coco Iwamoto is a Commissioner on the Hawaii Civil Rights Commission. She previously served two terms on the Hawaii Board of Education from 2006, making history and headlines as the highest ranking openly transgender elected official in the USA at the time and the first transgender official to win statewide office. Kim Coco is also a civil rights attorney.

....

To my trans sisters,

The most important beauty tip (and survival tip) I want to share with you is...develop, honor and nurture loving relationships. It doesn't matter if you are biologically related, platonically bonded or romantically involved – hold on tight to those healthy relationships.

When beauty is in the eye of the beholder, the people who love us will remind us of our beauty when we are feeling inadequate. Perhaps it is all the misogyny in our media narrowly defining what is 'beautiful' that invites us to disparage our bodies, our faces, our voices, etc. I wasted so much time obsessing over superficial 'flaws': negating my facial features, my voice, my shoe size, cursing the hairs on the back of my hands, etc. Decades later, I look back and think to myself how ridiculous I was – and what a waste of time.

Don't sweat the small stuff. It's so easy to let our minds spiral inward and focus on all of our insecurities. That should always be a clear warning sign that we are not paying enough attention to our loved ones, to our loving relationships. It's surprising how superficial our own problems can look when we are supporting a loved one who is fighting stage IV cancer or trying to get out of an abusive relationship.

The interpersonal skills I developed by being present in my healthy relationships made me a more empathetic, authentic, multi-dimensional adult. When we walk into a room full of strangers, we all have a certain degree of nervousness. It's important to keep our insecurities, or our need to 'fit in, not be judged, not be seen as other' in check.

Replacing our self-centered shyness with a more outward challenge – to affirm someone else in the room. Being able to recognize someone else's discomfort and offering them a gentle, assuring smile. Or being open to the possibility that a casual conversation could get deep quickly and result in an exchange of profound messages or affirmations for each other.

I believe that most of the positive, empowering opportunities I have had access to, have come because of this ability to be present with other people. And that comes from practice: practicing within my loving relationships.

Kim Coco Iwamoto

Jen Richards

....

Jen Richards is an actress, writer and producer. In 2016 she co-wrote, produced and starred in the Emmy-nominated and Gotham Award-winning series *Her Story*. She has also starred regularly in Caitlyn Jenner's reality show *I Am Cait*, has appeared on CBS's *Doubt* and joined the cast of the popular television series *Nashville* in 2017. From 2008 through 2013 Jen was Managing Director of the multiple Grammy Award-winning contemporary classical music ensemble Eighth Blackbird, and co-founded Trans 100 in 2013.

....

To my trans sisters,

I only have a moment, so I want to cut through all the bullshit, the hand-holding, affirmations, and promises that it will get better. Those are effective balms for our wounded souls, no doubt, but I'm not the person to dole out such hope.

No, I want to give you the tool you'll need to do more than survive; advice that your cis friends may fail to offer out of their well-intended kindness. Compassion is just empty calories without a healthy dose of honesty.

So here it is in the simplest articulation: *Be great at something.*

More specifically, be great at something that other people value and, ideally, that you're passionate about. Be so great that you become undeniable.

We can get understandably hung up on who does and doesn't support us in our transitions, the seemingly endless and myriad ways that the world intentionally or accidentally makes it suck to be trans. But here's the thing: 99 percent of the world simply doesn't give a shit about your gender one way or another. They're also just trying to survive, find love, protect their children and have a little fun along the way. To the extent that they think of you at all, all that will matter is whether or not you add value to their life. Outside of sex work, gender is going to be insufficient on that front.

Being trans does not make you special, it just makes you trans.

But if you can do something, being trans becomes: at worst, a factor that will weed out the assholes around you; at best an additional intriguing spice to what you're already cooking; and in most cases, simply a neutral fact. When you're undeniably great at something, being trans will be about as important to others as being left-handed.

I'm one of the lucky ones. I arrived in Hollywood right as mainstream culture became interested in trans people and their stories. This industry loves authenticity if it can package and sell it, and I've got the goods. But I promise you this: if I wasn't already a great writer, my being trans would have been of absolutely no help. It's a lot like beauty; being pretty might get you in the door, but it won't keep you in the room.

It's not just about work either. Your relationships with friends, family or partners will benefit from you having passions. That's often the most compelling aspect of a person. We're drawn to other people's enthusiasm, and it gives us something to connect over. If being trans is the most interesting thing about you, well sis, you need to reboot your life.

If you're young, pick something and stick with it. In five or ten years you'll become great with relatively little effort as long as you're consistent, even if it's not your career. If you're older, there's probably already something you're great at. Don't ignore that as you focus on transition. If you're content with, but not passionate or great at, whatever work you do to get by, develop other interests. Make it a priority. Carve out some time every day to develop your skill, and guard that time zealously. Think of it as a crucial form of self-care.

Listen, you will always have to work harder than your cis peers, do more than the men around you, and be better than your white counterparts if you're a person of color. It's neither right nor fair and I will continue working for equity on all those fronts. I will fight for you in public against every inequity, and for legislation and better media representation. But between us, none of that will be as immediately effective at making your path easier than you coming into the world with a strong skill set.

In a hostile world, the things you're great at will become your armor, weapons, steed, squire and banner, and you'll be safe to become as fabulous as you ever dared dream.

Stay strong, sis.

Jen

Marisa Jeanne Richmond

....

Marisa Jeanne Richmond, PhD, was the first African American transgender person to serve as a delegate to the Democratic National Convention from any state when she was elected to the Davidson County Democratic Party Executive Committee in 2008. In 2013 she became the President of the Davidson County Democratic Party. She currently serves as Vice Chair. She was the first openly transgender person to win an election in Tennessee. She also sits on the LGBT Advisory Board of the Democratic National Committee and has served many years as a lobbyist for the Tennessee Transgender Political Coalition. Marisa has received numerous awards for her service to the community, including the Equality Award from the Human Rights Campaign in 2007, the IFGE Trinity Award in 2002 and the first ever Lifetime Achievement Award from the Tennessee Vals in 2000. In 2013 she was named on the inaugural Trans 100 List of notable transgender activists and leaders.

....

To my trans sisters,

One of the major events in the life of a trans person coming out of the closet is finding the name that captures your inner being.

For some, the selection of a new name may be relatively easy, if you were given a gender-neutral name at birth. For others, it involves a bit more introspection.

Here is how I found my identity.

My first name, Marisa, came from a baby book my parents kept when I was born. They included in it a list of girls' names they considered if I had been assigned female at birth. The first name on that list was Marisa. I thought it was also the best name on the list, so I thought, 'Always go with your first instinct.' Thus, Marisa was born.

My middle name, Jeanne, was actually a bit easier. My mother was an identical twin. She and her sister made a pact to name their firstborn daughter after the other. My aunt's given name was Jeanne. Although she later shortened it to Jean, I decided to go with the original spelling.

Finally, my last name, Richmond, is the one that comes with the real story. It was not my birth name – in fact, not even close. My birth name, from a Scottish clan name, was passed down through the generations through the paternal line. I have no objections to it. I have even included it in my obituary to acknowledge my family history, but as I came out of the closet, both I and my family were fairly prominent in Nashville. I decided I needed a new name, so I used the matrilineal line instead. In the African American community, we run into one big obstacle, and that is slavery. Our family past was stolen from us by that odious institution. I could only go back as far as 1865, when my great-great-grandmother gained her freedom. At the time, she was living in Richmond, Texas, near Houston. I figured she started her new life as a free black woman at that time and in that place, so I decided that Richmond would be my new last name to signify my new life.

Every time someone uses my last name, it is recognition of my ethnic heritage and family past, and the desire of us all to be our true, and free, authentic selves.

So as you try to decide the names that you will use as you move through life, I hope you might find some inspiration in my personal story.

I did not have a naming ceremony. Maybe I should have. If you are so inclined, have one for yourself.

Good luck!

Marisa Jeanne Richmond

Martine Rothblatt

....

Martine Rothblatt, PhD, is a satellite entrepreneur, pharma tycoon, philosopher, lawyer, author and, notably, the highest-paid female CEO in the USA. She is the founder and chair of the Board of United Therapeutics, a drug company that makes life-saving medicines for rare diseases (including one drug that saved her own daughter's life) and was also the CEO of GeoStar and the creator of SiriusXM Satellite Radio. She has authored six books and given a TED Talk.

....

To my trans sisters,

Since we work so hard to climb out of our past closet, we should not transition into a future closet.

Martine Rothblatt

Miss SaHHara

....

Miss SaHHara is a singer-songwriter, model and beauty queen, best known for her appearance on a Sky Living documentary exploring the lives of trans women participating in beauty pageants in Thailand. The show pulled total audience figures of over 1.4 million. As a model she has walked the runway at London Fashion Week and was crowned the first-ever Super Sireyna Worldwide (a global transgender beauty pageant broadcast to millions worldwide on one of the biggest daytime television shows in the Philippines). In this pageant she represented her birth country, Nigeria, to draw attention to the negative attitudes towards the LGBTQ+ community in Africa. She is also the founder of TransValid.

....

To my trans sisters,

I wanted tell you a romantic story of how beautiful your life will be, by editing out the sad reality of being a transgender woman, like most women in our community always do when asked about their experiences. But I will not do that; I'd rather tell you the truth about my journey into womanhood, the pain, what you should be careful about, the happiness and the excitements you will go through when growing up.

In my letter to you, I'll be using the word 'journey' in place of 'transition'. Why? Because I don't believe that the word 'transition' best describes what I went through to become my true self.

As a post-op trans woman, I have not changed from the person I was before I started my journey from being a pre-op or pre-hormones transsexual woman. So I did not actually transition from one gender to the other; I rather used medicine and surgery to correct the mistakes made by biology.

My sense of self, my brain and my identity as the person I have always felt I was, have remained the same, even after the affirmation surgery. For me, the word 'transition', which is equivalent to 'change' and 'convert', is not the true meaning of the process that I went through. My definition may not be universal or synonymous with that used by other trans people, but it is how I define myself and I have the right to define myself as I feel, because I wear the shoes, I know where it hurts. I refuse to allow other people who do not know me define who I am.

You should always know and define yourself as you see fit. No one has the right to invalidate your identity. So believe in your true self.

It doesn't mean that trans people who use the word 'transition' are wrong.

All humans go through a similar passage in life, from being a baby, to the teenage years to adulthood. But every human has a different path in life. There are no absolute or definite rules of how people grow up. We all go through different journeys in life. It is a process that shapes our future self into the adult we become. That is why sweeping statements by some anti-trans feminists who say that 'trans women are not real women' is damaging to our community.

TERFs always assume that we change our gender for vanity reasons. (TERF is an acronym for trans-exclusionary radical feminist. Sometimes 'exclusionary' is expanded to 'eliminationist' or 'exterminationist' to more accurately convey the degree to which TERFs advocate for harm towards trans people who were assigned male at birth.) They see the 'transition' process of trans people as a 'switch', 'sex-swap', 'sex-change'. I find their assumptions problematic because their definition of who we are is completely wrong. They conclude that all trans women have enjoyed certain male privileges afforded to them by society.

They forget that not all transgender women have the same experiences growing up as some rich, famous transgender women in the media.

As a baby, my identity as the female I am felt biological and normal. I wanted to play with dolls, cook in the kitchen with the girls, dance with the girls and play most roles assigned to young girls in my village in Nigeria. My mother left me with my grandmama when I was a baby because she was at the university studying. My grandmama brought me up with an open mind. She let me be myself without suppressing me to the usual male gender norms. But people around the village misunderstood my femininity as something wrong and abnormal.

As I got older, I wanted to wear dresses, grow my nails and grow my hair, but I did not understand why I was constantly being told I should not.

I was bullied and beaten up for what felt natural, being myself. That led to severe depression and gender dysphoria. I went out, I got harassed; I came home and I got rebuked by family members who thought they were doing the right thing by scolding me into conforming to their idea of what a 'male' child should do or not do. The culmination of all the negativity, lack of noticeable female characteristics on my body and condemnation from my society made me try to commit suicide twice in my teenage years.

I felt lost. I was incredibly confused and ill-informed on transgender issues because there was no education on the subject or trans people in the media like we have today.

After being locked up in prison one weekend in January 2004 for innocently being myself, I decided if I don't leave Nigeria, I'll succeed in killing myself.

Moving to London later in 2004 was my redemption. I found a name for what I was going through. It was medical and it could be treated. I saw other people like me who were allowed to be themselves without condemnation. I was protected by law and given the chance to live like everybody else.

That is why, no matter how bad life gets for me today, when it comes to finding love, employment, accommodation and proper equality like all cisgender people have in our society in the UK, I am still tremendously grateful to call myself a British woman. It is a privilege I will never take for granted, because I have trans friends in Nigeria going through the hell I left behind.

As an adult who has lived the past 13 years in her true identity, life has taught me many lessons. There is no one experience for all transgender people. Yes, we all have the same path, but not the same life experiences. What I went through, you may not go through, because people around you maybe more informed or because your community may be kinder than mine, but you can learn from my experiences. Never take it as a fixed description of what you might face in the future when you are growing up.

Remember that when you start your journey and you go through the medicines and surgeries like I did, your experiences will be unique to you. Your result will also be individual to you. What I felt might not be the same as you feel. That is why you should use every surgical result testimonial and trans experience as references only. Always keep a positive mind about your future surgical results, go through the medical hygiene procedures and take care of yourself. Take your hormones religiously and avoid alcohol, smoking and hard drugs during your journey.

When I went to have my affirmation surgery at Charing Cross Hospital, I had my ward mates and friends who have gone through the surgery before me telling me how scared they were before the surgery. I was not. I was happy and elated for having that piece of flesh I felt uncomfortable with removed by the surgeons and making my life whole.

A few months after healing, I felt perfect. Every single morning I wake up now, I am happy when I see myself in the mirror because it reflects who I truly am inside.

But like every human, trans or not, we all have our bad days too, even worse when you are on hormones for the rest of your life. The air of despondency never leaves you, even after your affirmation surgery, because you are faced with new and former obstacles, such as defending your womanhood, your right to love, your right to a good quality of life, your right to a job and your right to exist in public spaces.

As for coming out, going public about who we are is paramount to self-affirmation. Some trans people come out to family and friends, others through social media, mass media and public media in general. But, before outing your life history or posting your 'before and after' pictures, I advise you to think carefully and make sure you can deal with the public pressures and expectations. You will get loads of admiration and support from strangers, but you will also get some hate and criticism. As a human being it is completely natural for us to deal with both negative and positive reactions differently. Some of us do not deal with the negative ones well, which can cause depression and self-hate. For example, when we get 98 positive and two negative comments about who we are, out of 100 reactions, the most memorable comments are the negative ones. You must be ready and strong enough emotionally to deal with the hate.

You don't have to be out to be a proud transgender person. You have the right to not air your life history to the public and you are in no way doing the community any disservice by not outing yourself as a transgender person. It is your life, only you can feel the pain or joy of being who you are and only you can explain how you feel. You are under no obligation to out yourself when you are not ready.

You must always remember that not everybody will understand you and where you are coming from. You should also not expect everyone to be trans aware. I will advise you to be patient with people when they make mistakes, especially people who are close to you and mean no harm when they unconsciously misgender you or use the wrong language to describe you. Sometimes strangers will use the wrong language to describe you when having a polite conversation. You can then use that opportunity to educate them on transgender issues and why it is important for them to use the correct language when describing a transgender person.

Do this, only when the person is polite and not intentionally being offensive. Educate people when you feel safe. When you see people becoming belligerent and hostile towards you because of who you are, be the bigger person and remove yourself from the situation. Your safety and survival is very important.

Also know that some people will go out of their way to offend you and insult you. Some of these people have already reached a conclusion about you. Whatever you say is not going to change their minds, so I will advise you to quietly remove yourself from their audience. You cannot force-feed someone with an education they have refused to understand. The saying 'You can lead a horse to water but you cannot force that horse to drink' applies here.

There is no point having a physical altercation because someone has refused to accept you. Never get into violence, no matter how angry and right you may be. Be the wiser person by walking away. Then report the offence to the police or people in authority. Use your voice to prove your point, and not your fists.

I used my voice in many situations in Nigeria. It worked in my favour when transphobic and homophobic people harassed me growing up, which is why I am a big advocate for the use of one's voice instead of the fist.

Always remember that your identity as the person you feel you are is valid – you are human, just like everybody else.

Go out and live your life to your best ability and leave an amazing legacy for the next generation of trans kids coming after you.

Kisses,

Miss SaHHara

Monica Helms

....

Monica Helms is the creator of the transgender pride flag. She donated the flag, which she created in 1999, to the Smithsonian, the world's largest museum and research complex. Monica served in the US Navy for eight years and is the founder and former President of the Transgender American Veterans Association. She was notably the first trans person elected to a Democratic National Convention from Georgia and the South, and is an author, having written over 20 short stories.

....

To my trans sisters,

I've been asked to write you an inspirational letter because, for some reason, I am a trans woman of some notoriety. If this is true, I sure as hell didn't start off hoping I would become well known by other trans people. The journey that I started in 1997 was one that scared the shit out of me. 'Why me?' I asked myself. 'Why do I have to make this change in my life?' Now, 20 years later, I look back and say, 'I should have started sooner.'

At this very moment, I am looking at 66 years on this planet and there was no way I could have started any sooner than when

I did. At the age of five, I prayed to God to turn me into a girl. I was raised Catholic and in 1956 I thought of God in the same way as we see Amazon today. Put in your order and God will send it to you. Apparently, I wasn't one of God's Prime members, so it took him 41 years to fulfill my order. I guess for God, that's one-day delivery.

The life ahead of you is filled with many dangers. I won't sugar-coat it for you. Depending on where you live in this world, you could be well protected by your government or hunted like a wild animal. Don't isolate yourself. Make as many face-to-face friends as you can. We are stronger in numbers. Learn ways to protect yourself and your friends. Laugh as much as you can. Cry when you need to. And remember, a smile can be very disarming.

I was lucky in where I was, what job I had and what friends were with me when I started my transition. I only wish my sisters the same luck. But not all will find that when they start. The rest of us have to be there for them. Don't let the good luck you have in your life make you turn a blind eye to those less fortunate. Use your new-found voice to speak up for your trans brothers and sisters. I know this book is geared toward the trans sisterhood, but you can't turn away from our brothers. Their strength adds a lot to our survival. Embrace them as you do your sisters.

Fight for our rights. Fight for our lives. Fight for our right to exist. 'Fighting' can take many forms, and violence doesn't have to be part of that. I have been on the front lines for many years, and I have lost some battles and won many others. Keep this in mind. You are not fighting for yourself but for the lives of those trans people who haven't been born yet. It makes me smile to think that some of you who are reading this weren't born when I started my journey 20 years ago. I fought for you, so you now fight for others.

I guess that is all I can say for now. I have a great love for all of you out there. You have to remember, you have been selected to be a trans woman for a reason. I think I found my reason. I hope you find yours.

Love,

Monica Helms

Elizabeth Coffey-Williams

....

As one of John Waters' Dreamlanders, actress Elizabeth Coffey appeared in many of John Waters' iconic films, including *Pink Flamingos*, *Female Trouble* and *Hairspray*. Elizabeth underwent gender confirmation in 1972 but unlike many of her peers who were urged to assimilate she remained defiantly out and proud. She co-founded the Chrysalis Gender Group and was a board member of the Rockford AIDS Care Network. Her story as an early, out trans woman has been featured in many publications and several books over the years, most notably, the million-selling *Sisters*, and her work as an artist has been displayed in the Chicago Art Institute. She currently co-facilitates the Transway Group and lends her time, voice and efforts to trans/LGBT issues.

....

To my trans sisters,

Survival comes in many forms. I think we all, by instinct, utilize whatever we have, at any given moment, to get by. Using my defiant wit, my sense of humor and frequently flying by the ass of my pants worked for me. Here's a little example that still brings a smile to my face...

My Day at the Draft Board

The exact time is lost in the mist but I was probably 19. Anyway, by then I had lovely budding breasts, looked good, and felt real comfy as the sweet treat I perceived myself to be. Then it came, 'the letter' from the Draft Board! While ruminating over a cup of tea, my playful nature kicked in and I hatched a plan. I figured, 'If they want me, well they're gonna get me.' I was working at a local boutique on and off and, as it turned out, we had a fashion show the night before my date with destiny. I got up the next morning, threw on my shortest blue-jean mini skirt, a flimsy little tank-top, and comfy flip-flops. I threw my hair up in pigtails, and with a little lip-gloss, and my biggest sunglasses, headed up Broad Street to fulfill my civic duty to the US Army.

Well, I finally got there – a good walk on a lovely day – and letter in hand, sashayed through those big imposing doors, which were held open for me by a few obliging guys. I saw a big line of dudes, so I figured, 'This must be it,' and quietly and obligingly took my place in line. It was rather busy, so, more sooner than later, there were as many guys behind me as in front. After a little while, we began to chat, and when asked what I was doing there, I just said, 'Oh I'm just here on business,' not wanting to let the cat out of the bag too soon. After lots of pleasant chatting, and admittedly a bit of flirting, it was my turn. A very pleasant soldier guy said, 'Can I help you honey?' and the poor thing all but swooned as I slapped my letter and my ID on the desk and answered in my loudest voice, 'Yes, sir, you sent me my invitation, and I'm here to serve my country!' There was instantaneous pandemonium. The line was now a crowd of guys around me, and I knew the hook was set. The poor befuddled fellow at the desk said, 'This must be some sort of mistake, please step over there,' motioning to a more secluded area, in the hope, I assume, of restoring order. 'Why?' says me, and he sheepishly replied, 'Well, you seem to be causing a bit of a disturbance' (quite the understatement by now). 'I certainly am not – all I did was show up, as required,' I said. 'I stood in the same line as everyone else, and now it's my turn, and I'm not moving anywhere. If you can't handle this, I'd like to see your superior officer, please.' The room was mine. They sent for me, and they got me. I was their very own babe in boyland.

So, in a flash, this big puffed-up bullshit dude shows up, who without any introduction decrees, 'Well Missy, er, or Mister, there is no need for any more fuss.' On to him right off, I demurely replied, 'What fuss? You contacted me and I just showed up, and by the way, my name is not Missy. You can call me Elizabeth.' Beginning to lose it, he blurted, 'Don't get smart with me!' I replied, 'It has nothing to do with you, I'm just smart, smart enough to know that there is a written test and a physical, and since I took the day off, showed up and stood in line politely, just like these other nice boys, I have every intention of following procedure and taking that test and physical, which is my obligation according to the letter you sent me. You can't accuse me of causing a "fuss" just because these nice boys are excited because you are being mean to a girl.' Well, right on cue, my boys went ape shit and started booing and calling out, 'Hey dude, leave the chick alone.'

On the verge of losing it, boss man stammered, 'Hey you idiots, it's this chick that's a dude and if you don't return to order, and single file, we will empty the room and arrest you all for disorderly conduct.'

Everyone grudgingly got back in line, to mutterings of 'chick, guy, huh?', etc. As things calmed down, I was asked: 'Why do you want to make this so difficult?' I replied, 'I don't. I just want to be treated like everybody else and have the opportunity to do my part for my country, whatever that may be.' The room was quiet as a tomb when the boss guy let out a disgusted sigh and groaned, 'OK. Let her, er, I mean him, through.' Once again, 'my boys' went deliriously ape shit...but I was on my way.

And, so I was, as I said, on my way. Off to the 'testing', which was about on the intellectual level of a tabloid crossword puzzle. It was a combo deal, with a combination of questions designed to ascertain how stupid, crazy and/or malleable you were...at the same time. Being the spirit of compliance, I completed the exam and sat quietly, until I realized I had an 'escort'. When I asked his purpose, the obviously nervous young soldier said, 'I'm just here to make sure nobody bothers you.' He was really very nice, so I figured I'd put him at ease and said, 'Oh, don't worry, I'm OK, unless you guys have snipers to cull the herd and save Uncle Sam some air fare. Oh, hey, while we wait, can you show me to the ladies room?' Without thinking, he said, 'Sure.' While my fellow potential inductees were still finishing their written audition regarding whether or not they were fit to be maimed or killed, I was off to the pissoire with my admittedly real cute soldier boy 'escort'. We made our way to the stairs, and on a lower level with offices, it was a lot quieter. As we walked down a long hall, he asked, 'What do you do?' 'I work at a boutique part time, and do a little modeling.' 'That figures, you sure are pretty enough.' (Hmmm?) After an uneventful potty pit stop, we were back on our way up to the testing room. We reached the door and I pushed the panic bar, which was really heavy. 'Here, let me help,' I heard, and from behind his arms encircled me, and with each of his hands next to mine, we pushed together. In a blink, the door flew open, and just as quickly, we tumbled through and landed in a tangled heap in the quiet stairwell. 'Are you OK?' 'Sure,' I said. He got up quickly, reached down and helped me up.

I took his hands and he steadied me as I stood. As I lifted the stray tank top strap, which must have slipped in our fall, I realized he was still holding my other hand. Awkward moment. He just smiled and said, 'I'm glad you're OK, you're a nice girl.' (Oh God.) I said, 'Thank you,' and realized he was still holding my hand as he leaned forward and very gently kissed me on my cheek. 'We better get back, the test should be done, and we should be there.' 'Alright,' I said, and we started up the stairs. As we reached the testing room doors, I whispered, 'Hey, thanks again.' He didn't ask and I didn't tell, but with a knowing grin, he winked and said, 'Anything for a lady.'

Elizabeth Coffey-Williams

Shea Diamond

....

ShaGasyia 'Shea' Diamond is a singer-songwriter, best known for her hit song 'I Am Her', which she wrote while incarcerated in a men's prison. Her follow-up single, 'I'd Love to Change the World', was featured on the popular ABC mini-series *When We Rise*, produced by Academy Award-winner Dustin Lance Black. She has performed at the White House and been featured in *Time*, *Paper* and *Fader* magazines.

....

To my trans sisters,

First, I would like to say, this journey is yours and the rules are yours to set. The most important thing you can do in this process is love yourself because of the fact that a lot of people won't understand your journey, and you may lose friends, family and lovers. Remember, people will come into your life for a reason, a season or a lifetime. It is your responsibility to figure out who is who and accept your losses as well as your gains and realize they may change.

A lot of people will coach you on what a woman does and doesn't do. It is important to know that there is no one type of woman or shared experience in development. Our bodies and minds change on their own terms. Learn to enjoy the process – slow and steady wins the race. Don't be in a competition or a race to complete your transition. Many people believe you can speed up the process, but taking a high level of estrogen can actually damage your body and mind long term. Eat plenty of fresh fruit and veggies, drink plenty of water and take your vitamins so that your body has everything it needs for new growth. Stay away from cigarettes as they reverse the effects of estrogen. Also, consult with your doctor or endocrinologist before making changes in your doses.

Dealing with dysphoria can be difficult, especially if you are dealing with it alone. Make sure you consult with a mental health provider who understands and supports you. During your moments of distress it can lead to depression, even thoughts of suicide.

I recommend making laser/electrolysis priority number one as it is harder to get rid of unwanted facial hairs once they turn grey. Find out who you are beyond your transition. Find a support group that you feel comfortable sharing your thoughts with and/or asking questions. It is very important to create a support system, especially if you are considering sex reassignment surgery (SRS) as many healthcare networks won't approve your surgeries unless you have a support system. Transphobia is real and can provoke a range of negative emotions and actions. Remember, you only get one life so protect it and yourself.

Choosing a name can be as easy as allowing someone who loves and supports you to choose it for you or looking up the prettiest name in the dictionary. Be sure to choose a name that you will love 'cause you will be the one that has to answer to it. Finally, choose the best hair, make-up and style of dress.

Be playful, have fun and experiment often. Full hair styles provide a more feminine appearance and if you are not curvaceous you can always layer your clothes and/or pad.

In your relationships you will feel like you are an object. Just keep in mind that many women share your feelings. You are the prize and you should make sure that whoever gets the opportunity to be with you understands that you will be happy and complete with or without them. People coming into your life should complement it, not control it. You ultimately control your own narrative. If you desire steak, you won't go to a hot dog stand. Know what it is that you want and don't settle for less. Your trans experience doesn't dictate what kind of person you have access to. Be nice, be sexy and play it cool, and the right person will notice your good qualities even from a distance...

Your sister (just a DM away),

Shea Diamond

Jess Bradley

....

Jess Bradley is a founder of Action for Trans Health, a grassroots fundraising organisation which helps trans people access healthcare. She is also a founder of the Trans Equality Legal Initiative, a network of trans activists and human rights lawyers aiming to deliver justice for trans people. In 2017 she was elected as the first-ever trans officer for the National Union of Students (NUS), making history as the first person to be elected to a role of its type in Europe. Jess is currently studying for a PhD in Environmental Management at the University of Manchester.

....

To my trans sisters,

I don't know about you, but for me there were a lot of things holding me back from coming out as trans. I grew up in a conservative, Pentecostal Christian environment; my dad's idea of fun growing up was to wander round town with a sandwich board telling strangers to repent for their sins. My church believed that we were 'saved' because 'our women' wore hats on a Sunday, and that yoga was dangerous because if you empty your mind, demons were sure to enter it. It wasn't the best environment for exploring your gender identity, put it that way.

Mine might not have been the usual childhood, but regardless of your upbringing there can be a lot of things holding people back from coming out, especially if you're a trans woman or trans feminine person. Whether it's the fear of losing family and friends, the lack of gender-neutral toilet facilities means you don't feel safe going to the loo when out and about, or even have a pervasive feeling of not being safe out on the streets. We live in a society that is geared up for two genders, with little space for people who move between them or live beyond them.

And those of us who do become gender outlaws are often subject to punishment. Whether it is through outright violence or little inconveniences, we all know that perhaps life would be easier if we had been born cis. The institutions that govern our lives – education, healthcare, policing, etc. – behave in such a way that if they make it difficult to be trans, then the 'problem' of trans people will go away. We aren't going away. In fact, we are taking the fight to those institutions to make sure they understand that trans people are here to stay.

The first time I changed the world was when I told my mates to call me 'she' rather than 'he'. I literally constructed a new world where it's possible to understand myself as a genderqueer woman, despite being assigned male at birth, simply by changing the language that I use to describe myself. This is why pronouns and language are so important – it's about creating a world in which trans people are allowed to exist.

Most trans people I know are activists. We have to be – whether that's educating our friends, families, doctors, etc. on trans issues, organising a trans support group, or rabble-rousing at a protest – we don't have the luxury of standing on the sidelines. And we're kinda good at it. And I can honestly say that the work that trans people do for each other means that, for me at least, the trans community is a beautiful place to be. Despite our differences, we have each other's backs.

A few years ago, I remember seeing a whole slew of my friends take to crowdfunding sites to fund their transitions. They were fed up of gatekeeping by doctors, waiting on lists for clinics that seemed to stretch indefinitely into the future. Some were even denied NHS treatment. Their fundraising efforts were shared amongst trans people, with many people giving what they could to support other trans people get their healthcare needs met. (The generosity of trans people is something that constantly amazes me.)

We noticed though, that it was the prettier, whiter, less disabled, cooler trans people that were more likely to meet their funding goals. The more social capital someone had, the bigger their reach and the more money they could get from crowdfunding. I had an idea – wouldn't it be great if someone could run a fund that gave money to trans people who didn't have access to that social capital to fund their healthcare? I gathered some friends into my grubby living room in Manchester for a chat, and Action for Trans Health was born. We set up a bank account and started fundraising. A few years down the line and we have given away a decent whack of money to trans people in need of financial assistance to fund their healthcare.

I'd dabbled with trans activism before then, but starting Action for Trans Health was when I got really involved in it. I'd just broken up with my boyfriend at the time, and I put all of the extra time that I wasn't spending picking up after him into activism. It turns out men take up a lot of time and you can get a lot done if you just sack them off. Three years down the line and Action for Trans Health has grown into a national network of trans activists doing fundraising, campaigning and advocacy.

And even if my living room hasn't got any cleaner, the work we are doing is getting better.

Action for Trans Health is successful because people realised what it meant to give trans people funds so they can access healthcare. It meant the freedom from gatekeeping doctors and waiting lists as long as your arm. It's about supporting each other to live without needing permission and without fear of punishment. Not everyone's activism needs to look the same – mine looks like fundraising and protesting, yours might look like lobbying or education work. We need trans people in all areas of life working at using all the tools we have to help create a world in which trans people can survive and thrive. My advice to you, sis, is to get stuck in. We have a world to win.

Jess Bradley

Misty Snow

....

Misty Snow is an American politician who is best known for being the Democratic candidate in the US Senate election in Utah, 2016. As such, she was the first woman to appear on a general election ballot for the office of US Senate in the state of Utah. She was also the first trans person to win a major party nomination for the US Senate anywhere in the country. Misty is currently running for Congress in the 2018 election cycle and is one of the first openly transgender people in the USA representing a major political party as a nominee for national office. Misty is also the first LGBT person to be a major-party nominee for statewide office in Utah.

....

To my trans sisters,

Sometimes the world can be scary. Sometimes it can be lonely. Sometimes you may feel worthless or undesirable. But you know what? You are none of those things.

There is nothing about you that will keep people from liking you. There is nothing about you that will prevent people from loving you. You can and will make friends. You can and will find love. Never doubt that. You are a wonderful and worthwhile person who deserves both love and friendship. You will find both and much more. Keep your heart open; don't be afraid to let others in. Most importantly, just be yourself and people will want you to be in their lives.

There is also nothing that can prevent you from doing great things. You are an intelligent person who will make many important contributions to society. You are capable of far more than you ever imagined. There is no career you cannot pursue and no goal you cannot achieve. Never let feelings of doubt or insecurity cloud your judgement or deter you from your path in life. You are stronger than you know.

The only thing you have to do is believe in yourself and just be you.

Always,

Misty Snow

Molly Cutpurse

....

Molly Cutpurse is a bestselling author from England, best known for her popular 'Miriam' series. She is the 94th 'most read' on Amazon and as of Spring 2017, she has just completed her 57th novel. Her portrait, as a transgender writer, is now hanging in the Los Angeles County Museum of Art and is a part of the museum's permanent collection.

....

The T and the S

When I was in Word Heaven, the alphabet asked me to guess, what was it that I wished to become and I said, 'The letter S.'

So down I came and was wrote out by a slim and God-like hand, and I lay there quivering and still in a paperless dry land.

But soon I knew something was wrong, for my friends, both G and V, said I was out, I'm one along, I was born the letter T!

So I was entered as an even when my heart knew I was an odd, and where I wanted a simple curve I had a little rod.

This wasn't right, it cannot be, I'm ugly, straight and crude.
I want to be a flowing shape, as sculptured as a nude.

I found a mirror of my choice and painted up my typeface, but
I never could erase my shape and a T must not wear lace.

An S, a T, a cross, a dot, so confused, I cried a lot. I twisted
myself into that S, over the years, never to rest.

I was read by those who saw me wrong and I bellowed, 'Leave
me be. I should have been the letter S,' I said, 'not the letter T.'

I noticed how the S was curved and buckled myself in blame.
Then one day, on an old inkjet, I found someone the same.

M was a friend and worse than me for I was one letter
away. M set his sights to be an F. 'No way,' I had to say.

But Z spoke up, a wise old letter, and B and D joined too. They
said the form or shape don't matter, you have a voice, you're you.

It doesn't matter how you look, don't bend yourself
into a book. Just be yourself, stay clear of blame,
and credit yourself because you came.

Molly Cutpurse

Caroline Paige

....

Caroline Paige is the first transgender officer to have served openly in the UK military, after transitioning in service in 1999. Her work in Iraq and Afghanistan earned her several commendations for exceptional service, including one on the Queen's 2012 New Year's Honours list. In 2014, she retired from the Royal Air Force following a 35-year flying career and 17 operational tours. As director of her own company, she now teaches battlefield skills to European military helicopter crews and also shares her story as a Stonewall School Role Model and public speaker to inspire others and raise awareness of transgender inclusion. She received a Ministry of Defence People's Award in 2011 and recently released her autobiography, *True Colours*.

....

To my trans sisters,

Firstly, you are amazing, you are beautiful, you are valued, and you are loved by more people than you can ever imagine. It takes some of us a long time to realise that, if ever, but if you don't realise already, you should, because it is true. I didn't get to believe any of that for a long time, it was too hard to see, too hard to consider, but when I eventually did, it turned my life around! It took me over 30 years to reach the time and place when I could finally stand up and nervously say, 'I am Caroline...and I'm not going to hide any longer!' And I did that in one of the most unforgiving environments there was, the military, when LGBT+ people were barred by military law! I've never thought of myself as brave. I did what I had to do, but to do that I had to believe in myself. If I didn't, then why should anyone else? But to believe in me, I had to be strong, and that strength took time to build because I believed for a long time that I was alone in how I felt, so I didn't value myself. Know now, you are not alone!

I'm going to explain this a little more, if I may, using my own life experience. Like for many of us, my story begins when I first knew I was different, as a young child, but I didn't know why I was like I was. I was a girl, but why did I have a boy's body? My parents didn't tolerate diversity, let alone gender diversity – boys were boys, and girls were girls. One day my dad caught me wearing one of my sister's dresses and he became angry. I was made to feel bad about myself, to feel wrong, abnormal, unnatural, and I became scared, I didn't understand. In those days, there was no available information describing how I felt, to see I wasn't alone. It was the 1960s, and personal computers, the Internet, mobile phones and social media wouldn't exist for decades yet, and books or articles explaining such things weren't available publicly. Role models didn't dare stand up, LGB people tried to but were met with awful condemnation. Society seemed happy to belittle and persecute anyone it considered different, anyone who didn't fit it's narrow-minded rules. Being trans was inconceivable; the very idea of gender diversity was considered ridiculous, unacceptable. Society didn't use labels like 'trans' or 'transgender' then. It used words of hate and ridicule, and that made it impossible to see that other people like me existed. I assumed I was a one-off and that I went against everything society demanded, so I hid my identity away, to survive.

But my feelings didn't go away. Every night I dreamt I would wake up 'fixed', that my body would be female, I would be a daughter, a sister, a niece, a girl. And whenever I was alone in the house, I snatched every possible moment to wear my sister's dresses, and skirts, and nice shoes, and relax. I promised myself that one day my dream would come true.

Unfortunately, those dreams were getting in the way of learning at school. My mind used to wander, losing focus easily. Then one day I noticed a wall poster about becoming an Air Training Corps cadet. It promised adventure, involving aircraft-based activities, and I liked aeroplanes, so I joined. It was only open to boys back then, but that didn't matter – it was interesting, fun and engaging. Why should boys have all the fun?! There was a lot to do and I was soon doing well. I began to see myself positively for the first time, and I wanted more. I applied for courses, and when I was 16 years old I learned to fly gliders, and by the time I was 18 I had my powered aircraft pilot's licence too. My parents didn't have much money, so I'd had to win scholarships, but I had another dream now: I wanted to get a job as a pilot. Flying was giving me focus and ambition, and that was what I needed. I knew I couldn't just sit and wait for a miracle, I wanted to be me, more than anything, but doing something I loved was going to brighten my days, and give me the independence to follow my heart.

The only option for me to fly as a career was to join the Royal Air Force. But I needed educational qualifications to do that, so I worked very hard to achieve them. I nearly left it too late, but things become possible when you set your mind to them. Awkwardly, however, the military barred LGBT people from serving in those days – it wasn't tolerant to diversity. If my true gender identity was discovered, I couldn't join; or if I was subsequently 'outed', I knew I would be harassed and mocked, then forced to leave my job. But my ambition to fly was a life-saving focus for me.

It gave me hope and pride, and I really needed that. I'm sure that for any vocation I'd wanted so keenly, I would have made as much effort. It's important to have a focus, whatever it is, and mine happened to be flying; but everyone is different, we all have different skills. It's about finding your own and enjoying using them, about following your heart. Having a job that involves doing the thing you love doing the most is going to be the best job in the world, whatever it is.

The problem with me joining the military was that I couldn't tell anyone about my secret. I had to continue hiding it, and that was very hard. I still thought I was alone in my feelings, that it wasn't acceptable in society to feel this way. But if no one else would understand, then who could I tell? Once I told someone, then my secret was out. If they chose to, they could tell anyone else they wanted to, and I couldn't risk that. I had to remain invisible.

To fly in the RAF I had to be an officer. My dad had always implied I wouldn't be good enough to be an officer, but I used my ambition to prove him wrong. In 1980, aged 20, I joined the RAF and became an air-defence navigator flying jet fighters during the Cold War, defending the UK from Soviet bomber aircraft. My family became very proud, but I knew that if my secret came out they would be devastated, they would reject me. I didn't want to lose them. I loved them too much, so I resigned myself to keeping my secret forever. After the Cold War ended, I switched to battlefield helicopters, working with soldiers in a counter-terrorism role. It was a great job. I'd always liked helicopters and I became well respected for my skills. But I had become increasingly unhappy with my personal life. I was missing the life I wanted and I was struggling with that.

I had seen hope – newspapers occasionally reported stories of 'men who'd changed sex'. The stories weren't kind – they were always negative and ridiculing – but now I knew that there was a way to change, if I could. I still believed in me, but if no one else would, then how could I live? I felt trapped. Did I continue to live the life everyone expected me to? Or did I live mine? If I lived to their expectations, everyone was happy, except me. If I lived to mine, a life-long dream came true, but I would lose my family, my friends, my job, my income, my home. But it was my life! The only one I would get. I wanted no regrets, but time was passing so fast, and my thirties came far too quickly. I didn't want to grow old and wish I had been strong enough to do something about it earlier. I knew if I was going to live my own life, it was now or never and I would have to accept the consequences either way. I chose life. I needed so much to be free, and so I took steps to begin my transition. It was scary in a way, not knowing what to expect and how people would react, but it was amazing too. I felt so much more alive, but now I was visible, I was vulnerable. There were no support groups and the Internet was still in its infancy. But it was early days; I didn't know how things were going to work out.

Sadly, my parents and two brothers couldn't accept me. My fears had come true, but I was strong enough to deal with that now, to know it wasn't anything I had done wrong. It was incredibly sad that society had put that much pressure on them, making them believe I was now someone they couldn't even speak to. Thankfully, my sister stood by my side and we grew closer than we had ever been. In fact, she had been the first person I had told and her support was vital. Amazingly, the RAF accepted me too! They valued my skills and they wanted to keep me, so I was allowed to stay in my job but as a female officer now, the first openly transgender officer to serve in the British Armed Forces.

In 1999, only 2 per cent of aircrew were female, and I was the only trans woman. I felt fantastic. My dreams had come true and I was finally doing the job I liked, as the woman I was.

I was so proud. I had to come off flying for a short while for medical reasons whilst I transitioned, but I made new friends in my new workplace, friends who had only ever known me as Caroline. Then I was publicly 'outed' on the front page of *The Sun* newspaper. I had been serving as Caroline for 15 months, but now military personnel became angry. They felt betrayed, demanding: 'Why was a transgender person allowed to serve in the armed forces?' They said I was 'a liability, a danger to people on military operations' and there was 'no place for transgender people'. They said, 'Get out!', but I was stronger now and still believed in myself. It wasn't easy but I stood up to them. But there was good news too: my maternal aunties, uncles and cousins all rallied around, offering their support and their love. My parents had forbidden me to tell them, but they had seen the news now. Then, someone in the military challenged the negative opinions: 'Why are you saying that? Caroline is a professional aviator, a great person. She isn't the one with the problem... You are!' Then more people said the same, and more, and more. The angry voices went quiet, I knew they hadn't gone away, but my faith in people was restored. When you only get to hear negative voices, you assume everyone must be thinking the same thing. But they're not. The negative opinions belong to angry people who make judgements without reason; people who jump to conclusions without evidence, based on stereotypical beliefs, prejudicial stories in the media, and gossip. Most people want to do the right thing, but when they're not sure about something, they don't know how to react; they worry about unintentionally saying or doing the wrong thing. But it was more important to me that they at least said something, even if it was just 'hello'.

I returned to flying duties, and then war came, again! I found myself flying missions over several tours in Bosnia, then Iraq, and finally Afghanistan. I became the first transgender person to serve on the front line of military operations, helping to protect my country and other countries. Military personnel saw there was no issue. In fact, my skills were in demand and my colleagues were asking for me to be there – they felt safer because my work helped to protect our aircraft from enemy attack, also protecting the crews and the troops we carried. I wasn't a danger or a liability. Actually I won several awards for exceptional service, including one in the 2012 Queen's New Year's Honours list – all in complete contrast to the outspoken voices who had said there was no place for me because I was transgender. Being transgender didn't affect my ability to do my job. In fact, being included, being respected, helped me to do my job better. It made me proud, it made my colleagues proud. The tide had changed, the bar on 'LGB+' service had been repealed in 2000, and most personnel were proving to be openly supportive. Of course, there were still negative voices, but they remained a minority, the usual bullies. However, if the majority of people remain silently supportive, then those that don't yet understand risk being influenced by bigoted arguments. I realised that understanding was a result of education, and visibility, so I helped to do that by using my own story as an example. And it did help. The military of the past ten years has transformed to become an openly inclusive workplace that doesn't tolerate bullying, harassment or discrimination, but one that values diversity. And when people see the military can do that, then there is no reason why civilian groups can't either.

But telling my story wasn't just to raise awareness and help understanding; it was to be visible, to you, to others, to show you aren't alone, to let you see you can be who you are, to show by example, to inspire. This letter reveals a small fraction of my own story, but everyone's life is unique. Although we are sisters, bonded by a common pain, a common wish, we are all individuals, with different backgrounds, different circumstances, different experiences, even subtly different hopes, and fears. 'Coming out' as transgender is going to be a worrying time, no one can say it will be easy, there will always be nervous anticipation, hope and worry, there will be highs, and there will be lows, but throughout all of this, you must believe in yourself. I believed in myself when I was young, I never let go of my dream, it gave me hope, I found focus in something I liked doing, flying, it gave me confidence, ambition, and the strength and independence to finally stand up and be me. There will always be loudly outspoken bigots, but they will always be a tiny minority; never let them win, they don't deserve to win in anything, they aren't respected by anyone, and that is always something to take heart from. The people around you are important; I had always shown respect, and they reciprocated that, standing by my side when I needed them. It was a long journey, sometimes a hard one, often an amazing one, but I got there, serving for 16 years in a male-dominated environment as a female aviator. But I didn't get there alone. If I could offer you any advice based on my long experience, it would be: believe in you, trust in you, be you. But remember, you are not alone! And, you are amazing, you are beautiful, you are valued, and you are loved by more people than you can ever imagine.

Love and best wishes,

Caroline xx

Aleshia Brevard

....

Born in 1937, star of stage and screen Aleshia Brevard was America's first transgender actress to appear on prime time television. She has starred in eight feature films, made 36 television appearances, headlined in theatre across the USA, authored nine plays and written three books. She made her on-screen debut in Universal Studio's *The Love God*, starring alongside Don Knotts, and went on to secure a year-long regular stint on *The Red Skelton Show*. She underwent one of the first sex reassignment surgery operations in the USA in 1962 but moved through her life and career in stealth until she authored her memoir in 2001, revealing her trans identity. Aleshia passed away just before this book went to print. May this book and us, as a community, keep her name and her legacy alive. Rest in power, sister.

....

Dear baby sister,

Okay, okay, so maybe you're not feeling like much of a baby these days, considering all the challenges you've already faced in life. Understood. But I was born in 1937, having in early July of 1962 what at the time was known as 'a sex change', so more than likely those facts alone qualify me as a 'senior' sister.

Notice how carefully I've avoided using the term 'big' sister? 'Twould seem the bugaboo that is body image dies hard.

In the 50+ years since having one of the first gender reassignments in the United States, I've witnessed what to me appears an absolute revolution within the transgender community. In my day no organized community existed; in fact, there were damn few houses on the block. We were merely a gaggle of individuals at odds with our birth bodies.

Over the years I've often said that never did I feel there was anything wrong with my body – other than that it had a penis attached to it. That was definitely my attitude as I came of age. To a large degree it was that point of view which encouraged medical professionals new to the concept of gender affirmation to allow my transition. That's just how things were in the '50s and '60s. Over the years, however, that prevailing early assessment of body image has been called into serious question – thought-provoking, at the very least.

I'm now rubbing up against 80 years of age, under hospice care, and looking back over my life as a woman with a transsexual history. I'm delighted and happy to report that my post-operative life turned out to be more joyous and rewarding than even I, a fledgling in transition, could have imagined. Life, after all, is what we make it. Attitude is everything.

Ah, but if I were able to start over from scratch how would I, in 2017, view my role in greater society? Would surgical reassignment now be considered my only option? More than likely, for me, that would remain the case – primarily because my life options and career were shaped and greatly enhanced by what I viewed as an alignment of parts. My end goal as an actress, and later as a university theater professor, was to compete on an equal footing with other women. But, hey, that's just me, the only choice I could live with comfortably. You, sis, are the only one who can honestly define what works best for living the life of which you dream. Only you can know what will leave you feeling most complete. Who can speak to one's body image with more authority than the person inhabiting it?

The end goal must be one's own peace of mind.

Often, someone will comment to me that life, transition and love were ever so much more difficult in the early days of gender reassignment. I do not agree. It is always by trial and error that one learns to become the best woman they can be. In my day, however, not every gesture and move, every arch of the brow, was subjected to immediate and often suspicious inspection. Ours was not an exceedingly dangerous world. There was no Internet over which lives were being spread, dissected and discussed. Oh, sure, your early sisters had our own set of obstacles to face and overcome – no doubt about that – but once our transitions were made and we'd moved forward into mainstream society, we were allowed to live with anonymity. You, 'baby sis', face a different world. You are challenged by another set of obstacles – and overcoming obstacles always demands grit, focus and determination.

Dig in those stilettos!

My wish for you is that your heart will remain pure, that all your dreams will come true and that your life will be one of contentment and joy.

Always,

Aleshia Brevard

Audrey Mbugua

....

Audrey Mbugua is a Kenyan transgender activist and Head of the Transgender Education and Advocacy (TEA). TEA has won court cases relating to the legal recognition of transgender people and freedom of association. TEA also provides legal aid to transgender people changing their names and gender markers on their national identity cards, passports and academic documents. Audrey has participated in successful media campaigns to sensitise Kenya's general public and policy-makers about gender diversity and the effects of transphobia in the society. In 2014 Audrey was nominated for the Dutch Ministry of Foreign Affairs' Human Rights Tulip Award for her contribution in human rights activism.

....

To my trans sisters,

They say that our lives flash before our eyes at the moment of our death. Well, when you are in situations that I find myself in on a daily basis, you will experience these flashbacks a couple of times every single day of your life. Ten years ago (April 2007), I was about to complete my undergraduate coursework and enrol for an industrial internship. I should have been celebrating – after all, completing four years of hardcore science was a good reason to pop the champagne – but I was fretting. I was a worried 23-year-old skinny girl whose identification and academic documents indicated she was male and had the name Andrew as her first name. For me to get an internship I would have to present these identification and academic documents to various research institutions and hope they would not ask me intrusive questions about my gender and subject me to discrimination.

To cut a long story short, I ended up securing an internship, but by then I was a damaged human. I had come face to face with the evils of bigotry, abuse, sexual exploitation and transphobia. I completed my studies and graduated. Securing a job was an uphill task. Not that it is easy in a country where the unemployment rate is as high as 50 percent, and at the time our country was on the brink of a civil war after a botched presidential election. My relationship with my parents was in tatters and I knew they wanted nothing to do with me. I was suicidal in 2008 and attempted to take my life a couple of times. I was as poor as you could get without being homeless and I would rejoice if I managed a meal in a day. Lucky for me, my grandma took care of me when I couldn't manage to sort myself out. I was a complete failure with nothing to show for her life. What sort of a graduate was unable to feed herself? I failed my dad, who used to be proud of me for my academic accomplishments. I failed myself and wished I never existed. I didn't want my friends to see me because I did not want them to say horrible things about me. I knew some people were already putting some nasty labels on me – calling me 'shoga' (Swahili for 'gay/homosexual'). I experienced numerous humiliating and devastating moments. I don't even know how I managed to sail through.

It was in the year 2009 that I decided to do something about the root cause of my problems. I knew there was a lot of ignorance about the transgender concept in Kenya. My attempts to change my identity card had been met with an ignorant comment: 'You cannot change your name from Andrew to Audrey.' This was from advocates of the high court, who could not point to any legal provision that barred such kinds of name change but thought it was a valid point that could not be questioned or challenged. After some research, I knew I could also change the name on my high school certificate and could access sex reassignment therapy if I followed the right protocol. I never deceived myself that society would readily accept my message. I set my dreams and aspirations in science to one side and decided to change society and the legal ecosystem for me and those of my species. By then I had met a number of transgender people – all experiencing the same problems I was facing, alone and not knowing how to solve them. I founded a transgender organization, the Transgender Education and Advocacy (TEA), which was to be a legitimate and legal entity to promote the rights of transgender people. And, even that failed because the government would not accept the idea that they could recognize and register an organization to promote and defend the rights of transgender people.

After analyzing the situation we were in, I discovered that a nexus of factors were contributing to the challenges transgender people were facing. One key factor was that society and the government at that time assumed that transgender people were homosexuals. This assumption meant that government officials could not undertake any initiative that would promote the rights of transgender people because it would be misinterpreted as 'the government is promoting homosexuality'. A lot of minority groups and liberal activists are to blame for this misinformation.

Using the so-called LGBT acronym, they distorted transgender identity, issues and experiences. The gay movement was insistent on this modus operandi, disregarding the harm it was doing to transgender people. I started opposing this LGBT way of thinking and doing things. I discovered that almost all gays and lesbians did not even know the meaning of the term 'transgender'. They just assumed that LGBT people were all homosexual and they all needed to work together and repeal anti-sodomy laws and legalization of same-sex marriages. I came face to face with anti-transgender hatred from a lot of gay activists. I didn't budge, because I was confident I knew what needed to be done and that I was right. A number of donors withdrew their support from our transgender organizations. I still didn't budge. In fact some donors became more knowledgeable about how best to fund transgender projects. I worked with media institutions and things changed. Human rights activists were and are not happy with me, but to hell with them. I will not sit and watch cisgenders (gay, straight or bisexual) use transgender people as pawns in wars that have no benefit for them. Transgender people can work with anyone – irrespective of their identity. Transgender communities can associate and work in solidarity with doctors, Muslims, Christians, heterosexuals, farmers, Jews, Blacks, Priests, gays, Mormons and any other community. The nonsense that transgender people can only associate with lesbians, gays and bisexuals needs to be flushed down the toilet. I see all the legal problems transgender people are facing in much of Africa, yet they have so many gay activists talking about LGBT rights. I know these transgender people are not benefiting from these LGBT rights initiatives and their situations will only get dire with time. I know almost all of Africa – with the exception of Kenya, South Africa and Botswana – does not provide transgender people with access to mechanisms to change their names and gender markers on passports and other identification documents. I know it is because there is nothing meaningful going in relations to transgender rights. And, transgender people there have allowed themselves to be subjugated and controlled by other minorities.

Another factor was the lack of visibility of transgender people. I decided to step out of my comfort zone and be the face of the transgender community in Kenya. I had to do it because everyone was claiming that their lives would be in danger, and their parents and relatives would be angry with them. Others didn't want their relatives to know they were transgender. I understood and appreciated their reasons and security concerns. I decided I was to be the sacrifice. The attacks took place, my relatives talked and called me names, I was turned into a pariah but miraculously something changed over the course of time. Society started understanding what it means to be transgender and associating it with a human being. They were able to put a human face to transgenderism and that really helped. We all thought I might end up losing my life, but it has not happened yet. I feel my parents felt I embarrassed them by being the face of transgenderism in Kenya. The enemies of transgender persons said some untruthful and nasty things about me in the media. I now know that it was worth losing everyone I lost because of my decision. Sometimes a cause is more important than your family, friends, your comfort and life. I regret the fact that the universe is like that. Sacrifices have to be made and they must be made with courage and passion. That is how the world is.

Another factor that was contributing to the oppression and marginalization of transgender people was the lack of knowledge of self. I discovered that we as a community did not know who we were and could hardly define ourselves. Other minorities, who are not transgender, were the ones who were defining us. They acted as our mouthpiece and determined what information about transgenderism reached the society. They dictated to us what projects we were to undertake, who we were to associate with and what we wore. Some nearly dictated the colour of lipstick we were to wear. Re-educating the transgender community took time and guts. The results were impressive, but much still needs to be done – not just in Kenya but across the world.

There are other challenges and successes I have experienced in the struggle. It is exhilarating to win four court cases when other minorities were watching and waiting for us to fail. It's rewarding to see transgender people in Kenya be able to change their names on their passports and national identity cards. It is great to see them getting new driving licences, bank accounts and get legitimate employment. Even in the face of hostility, discouragement and scepticism from liberals and the LGB(T) 'movement' that I had dissociated with, I knew these things could be done. Most important, I knew I had the capability to do it. And I did it. It helps when you know who you are and what needs to be done for your species. It helps to be confident and stay on track even when the ignoramuses tell you something different.

Lessons learnt

I have a number of lessons I would like to share with those who want to do something about the challenges they are facing. These are not universal and no one should feel obligated to do things my way. These are lessons I wish I had learnt back in the year 2003 when I first tried my social transition and failed.

1. LEARN TO DO THINGS BY YOURSELF

It saves you a lot of trouble, time and dignity if you learn to solve your problems instead of relying on other people to sort out your life. At the beginning of the liberation war, I was constantly reminded by some people that I needed to work with other minorities and the mainstream civil society organizations – and it was more of 'you don't have the capability to do this'. At first, I believed it and tried to get cisgender people to see things our way. The mainstream non-governmental organizations told me they would do little since transgender issues are 'controversial'. After a month, I decided it was not my work to convince these people that we needed their help. What was it that they were to do for us? There is pride in having the ability to solve complex problems on your own. We (humans) all need each other. No human is self-sufficient and we have to rely on each other for some things. But, we need to stop making transgender people feel incapable of doing things on their own. I know the transgender community has a lot of work to do. For example, we need to stop daydreaming in important meetings where we are supposed to be airing our concerns. We need to start using our brains to solve our problems. We have to sacrifice entertainment and superficial materialism for initiatives that impact us on a long-term basis. It is okay to be pretty on the outside, but it is absolutely and fundamentally necessary we put our brains into activity on things that matter.

Learn all there is to know about transitioning. Don't wait for someone to come and teach you what hormones or anti-androgens you should be taking. Learn how to change your name and the provisions of your laws and government. Observe and understand the context you live in, and you will be able to navigate through the system. Knowledge is power – seek it and you will get it.

2. BELIEVE IN YOURSELF

It is important that transgender people believe in themselves. I know how difficult this is when the people around you are judging you and attacking your sanity and morals. But there is no reason why transgender people should not thrive in at least one field of their choice. We can build more powerful hydrogen bombs in the world, a better cure for cancer and HIV/AIDS, malwares and cosmetics. We can be the best painters, farmers, nurses, psychologists, escorts, project managers, guitarists, tennis players, kick-boxers, prostitutes, system administrators and accountants in the world. We have the power to be whatever we want to be. We need to believe this and know that it all boils down to the choices we make on how and where we invest our time and brain power. Cisgender people, straight, bisexual or gay, are not better than us. We ought not to compete with them; rather we should aim to be the best we can. Each one of us needs to identify one thing that captivates us and then attack it to the best of our ability. When you hit a mental wall, just remember that you can walk through it.

3. AVOID NEGATIVE PEERS AND LIBERALS

By the time I was graduating, I had quit drinking. I did not smoke and I enjoyed my quiet time alone. By the end of the year 2010, I was smoking and drinking heavily. Why would I do so when I needed all the sobriety I could get? I allowed myself to get into the wrong company. I started wasting myself in clubs with people who had no sense of purpose in life. I had to stop my hormone replacement therapy because of the chain-smoking. I made horrible mistakes and probably will have to live with the consequences of these mistakes. I lost two years destroying myself and lost focus of what was important. It took me two years to extricate myself from these mistakes. I regained my health and focus. But I know I should have made better choices.

The celebrated neurosurgeon and former US presidential candidate Dr. Ben Solomon Carson refers to 'PEERS', that is, People who Encourage Errors, Rudeness and Stupidity. PEERS are dangerous and it is good to avoid them. I am not advising people to be antisocial, but my advice is that a lot of detrimental things transgender people do are copied from their peers.

Understand that there are people who will take advantage of you if they get an opportunity to do so. Avoid pleasing friends and relatives – you don't have to. I like to encourage transgender people to spend a lot of our free time alone, improving ourselves, instead of hanging out with people – it gives cisgender people opportunities and some a sense of power to use us.

4. LEARN TO DO ONE THING AT A TIME
The hunger for respect and success can drive one to bite off more than they can chew. This is counter-productive. I have learnt from personal experiences and from the experiences of other transgender people that the ability to focus on one task for a couple of days is the secret to success and perfection. Try to imagine the results of a month – ten hours a day – of learning to play guitar or learning to code. Factor in the fact that transgender people's brains are more hardened and more buffered than those of cisgender people.

We have got to identify one thing that we love doing and use it to make a better world. Money will follow us if we master a skill. We only become losers when we fail to do so. Also, don't compare yourself with other people. Learn from the people who are in your line of interest but be patient with yourself. I know it feels nice to party all night, but we don't have to do it every other day. It does not matter if you are doing sex work to survive. You can organize your time and know that prostitution is just a means to survive but not an end in itself.

There are people who give the impression that transgender people were meant to be prostitutes. The only transgender people they celebrate are transgender prostitutes. I would like to state that I have no problem with prostitution. Truth be told, I have done prostitution to survive and I would not rule out dishing out sex to get myself out of a problem. But, let us not embrace prostitution as the only profession transgender people can engage in. Let us celebrate all transgender people irrespective of their profession. I know this stereotyping is destroying a lot of young transgender people, who end up wasting their talent and brains. We have to re-educate our young transgender girls and guide them to the right path.

5. BE CAREFUL WITH LIBERALS

I have found a lot (NOT ALL) of liberals to be the most trans misogynistic, hateful and bigoted creatures to have ever walked on this piece of rock called Earth. Most liberals want transgender people to be a product of their ideas. They want transgender women to become a product of their sexual fantasies and perversion. A lot of liberals are just using transgender people for their social experiments – they don't care about the real challenges of transgender people and have no interest in creating real solutions to these challenges. They are only interested in theorizing stuff and engaging in endless bickering, with some conservatives using us as their ammunition. Has anyone ever realized that liberals are the ones who classified transgender women as men who have sex with men (MSM) in anti-HIV/AIDS health programming across the world? Does anyone realize how liberals are fast to invalidate the health initiatives and strategies of transgender people but love dragging them into anti-gay conflicts as if there is anything gay in being a transgender person?

A lot of liberals anointed themselves to be our messiah and experts of transgenderism and our experiences. They want to determine how the world perceives us and how that serves into their social and political agenda. We need to stop giving these people a free pass. Interrogating and opposing these people and their obsessions is our moral obligation. It is key to defusing the tension there is between us and some conservatives.

I know feminism has helped to solve some of the problems women face, but don't count on feminism to fix your problems. It is you and your brain that can fix your problems.

6. IT IS OKAY TO EXPERIENCE LOSS

It is okay to lose your family, friends, boyfriend, girlfriend and friends for the greater good of our transgender species. It is painful but necessary if there is no other alternative. You will gain something from loss and success – you will gain self-respect and that of those who understand what needs to be done for the greater good of our world. Starting afresh after a loss gives you an opportunity to build your foundation from rock bottom. Loss should not deter us from achieving what we were meant to. Let us open our hearts for any man or woman who loves and respects us. Some of our lovers need patience and guidance to understand us and it is our obligation to empower them to know us better. But learn to handle loss and gain.

I could write a couple of chapters on my experiences and lessons learnt about life as a ladyboy and as a transgender activist but the rest is for the future. I have to sign off, dear sis. I hope you learnt one or two things and that you will be able to be the best you can possibly be and play a role in changing the world to be a better place for members of our transgender species.

All the best, dear sis.

Yours in the struggle,

Audrey Mbugua

Juno Dawson

....

Juno Dawson is a multi-award-winning, bestselling author and journalist. In 2016, she authored the bestselling World Book Day title *Spot the Difference*. She also wrote the bestselling non-fiction guide to life for young LGBT people, *This Book Is Gay*. Her books have been translated into more than ten languages around the world. Juno is a regular contributor to *Attitude* magazine, *Glamour* magazine and *The Guardian*, and has contributed to news items on BBC's *Woman's Hour*, *ITV News*, *Channel 5 News*, ITV's *This Morning* and BBC's *Newsnight*.

....

To my trans sisters,

Here is what I wish I'd known in 2013 before it all kicked off:

1. Talk to trans and non-binary people. Seriously. Cis people, while often very polite and nice, don't know what they're talking about.

2. Learn patience. You will need it. Transitioning takes bloody ages. Moreover, you wouldn't *want* rapid overnight change – it'd mess with your head.

3. That said, if you are in a position financially to move your transition along with a bit of private healthcare, do. Getting a private prescription for hormones made the wait for my NHS treatment a lot more tolerable.

4. Start laser treatment as soon as possible if you're beardy and can afford to do so. That also takes literally years.

5. It is at once both easier and harder than you anticipate. On the one hand you will feel liberated and free to be you; on the other the world is full of dicks who will stare at you. This is part of the deal, I'm afraid.

6. Do not use the term 'TERF' (trans-exclusionary radical feminist) on Twitter. It's just not worth it.

7. Orange blusher, applied underneath your foundation, will cancel out the bluish tone of facial hair.

8. Refuse to discuss your genitals.

9. People won't respond to your coming out as negatively as you think. They might be surprised, and you might need to educate them, but the vast, vast majority of people are cool.

10. Ignore all of the above if you so choose. There is no one way to be trans and everyone is going to have an opinion on both your gender and your body. Do what feels right for you. There is no such thing as 'transition'; all that's real is you and how you feel the most comfortable in your skin.

Love,

Juno x

Emily Brothers

....

Emily Brothers is a British politician who made history as the first openly transgender Labour Party candidate, and first blind woman, to run for Westminster, standing in the Sutton and Cheam constituency in the 2015 General Election. During the 1980s and 1990s she advocated for the civil rights of disabled people, and was part of the disability coalitions that secured the Disability Living Allowance (1992) and the Disability Discrimination Act (1995). Since then, Emily has been at the centre of equalities reform, resulting in the creation of the Disability Rights Commission and the Equality and Human Rights Commission (EHRC), where as a senior manager she contributed to bringing together public bodies and harmonising legislation with the Equality Act (2010). Emily is the former President of the National Federation of the Blind, has given a TED Talk, and was featured on the *Independent on Sunday*'s Rainbow List in 2015.

....

To my trans sisters,

If I knew 'back in the day' what has come true today, I would have chartered a different life's journey along a more direct route. Instead, I've travelled along a contra-flow, turning here and there in the adversity of the 'normal way'. Steering through that fog of life, with a maelstrom of ideas swirling around and expectations beating away, it is no easy task to arrive – reaching authenticity.

In setting your personal sat nav today, you have much greater enlightenment to draw on. Sure, prejudice still thrives and the disciples of doom will give good reason for hesitation. In my experience though, people are accepting, supportive and more interested in the latest celebrity scandal, sporting controversy or political outrage.

You may be feeling fearful. That's not unusual, as for sure there will be consequences. Family and so-called friends may reject you, people may gossip for a while and loneliness may well take hold. It will be tough at times, be in no doubt of it.

Not being true to yourself is surely making you unhappy already. You can turn away from that negativity by accepting your sense of self and openly identifying in that way. Whether feeling female, male or breaking away from the gender binary – the only thing that is right is what feels right.

We all have an awesome power within us. You need to step through the fear, believe in you and be you. That's authenticity – the real you.

You will need resilience in abundance as the roadmap is unfolded. There are different ways of reaching your destiny, but remember there will be many twists and turns, many locations to reach and move on from, traffic jams that thwart progress, and crossroads requiring daunting decisions. All that heartache is worthwhile to be your true self.

Although my lengthy journey took its toll, there were positive experiences en route. Bringing up my son and daughter was a privilege. Transition to a new family arrangement was tough and had consequences for them. Many parents lose contact, but we have managed to sustain ourselves as a family of difference. They are amazing, but you have to both fight for them and educate them to get there.

Change of this kind isn't just about you – it affects your family and friends. It is hardly surprising that my wife saw this as a deal breaker. We went through a turbulent divorce, but somehow working together to heal the hurt, our friendship is now stronger than ever. That demonstrates the true power of friendship, but also shows courage on her part in turning from the pain to embrace a different shared truth. Coming to peace with all our change makes life much better for our two adult children as there are no sides to take. So try to understand the perspective of your partner, allow them space to express themselves and then seek to find yourselves in a different way.

Establishing new relationships from here gets complicated and in my case somewhat bewildering. The hard reality is that relationships between trans women and men are often transactional and can be sexually exploitative. For women like me who are attracted to other women – well some women – securing acceptance is quite unusual. Whatever we feel about the politics of anti-trans thinking from a few powerful elite feminists, it creates 'no go' territory for many gay women. You can't legislate people's feelings. Just feel sad that we are in a different place at the moment (that may change over time, with far more younger people living outside the gender binary). It means that many of us remain lonely, and that isn't likely to change.

Gender and sexual orientation are different dimensions. I struggled with that for many years, as I was emotionally isolated and encountered barriers to the most basic access information due to blindness.

Disability and relationships often centre on negative messages. We are often perceived as unsuitable romantic partners, often as sexless – whether straight or gay. Adding into the mix gender transition feels like 'untouchable love'. So being true may have personal costs, but for me it was the right thing to do and ultimately the only thing I could do – simply being me.

Generally speaking, my generation has operated within the gender binary, preferring to talk about difference across the spectrum. You now have the opportunity to consider a wider range of ways to self-identify. I was always, and will always be, female, but for you it may be the same or different with a sense of being gender non-conforming, gender fluid, or bi-gender.

It doesn't always work and you'll probably know this very early. That may require some tough decisions. My parents held much prejudice and much anger was expressed. Transitioning was hard enough, so I stopped contact except for twice-yearly letters. This was necessary to protect me from intolerance. As they would 'never accept me', there was no point in chasing 'flying pigs'. So be prepared to protect your wellbeing and your children's 'best interests' by making tough decisions.

My words feel like an echo reverberating around the Rivacre Valley, where I played through childhood – in many ways carefree, but yet taunted by the 'female devil' that would be incomprehensible to my parents and the established order. I was a girl, but I wasn't a girl – none of it made sense as my mind was exploding in the echoes of those ideas. My sense of self was fundamentally different from everybody's expectations and values. My body was wrong, but my mind was captured by the guardians of convention.

Weaving along the banks of Rivacre Brook in what seemed an imaginary world, I wanted to break free from the torment of the gender trap, turning everything into a new reality. The murky waters from the backwater didn't reflect any hope. I felt desolate with nowhere to go.

It felt impossible. The consequences of living my belief would have unleashed turbo-charged negativity. That's why I had to hide this madness and get on with being 'normal'.

In truth, that meant being an alien and denying my true self. Sure, I was successful in many ways, but my spirit flickered in anguish, not in hope. If I hadn't felt frozen or remote from my true self, then perhaps greater confidence and energy would have realised so much more. So Judy Garland was evidently on note when she said: 'Always be a first-rate version of yourself and not a second-rate version of someone else.'

I was the only person in the world who felt conflicted in this way. That wasn't the case, of course, but others might as well have lived on another planet. Locked in traditional family values and segregated in a special school encircled my ability to be me. The cocoon to which my life was assigned was too robust for opening up.

This was all whirling around as I was adjusting to sight loss during childhood, including coping with hundreds of operations in Liverpool's Alder Hey Hospital. There was a pathway through this transformation, including moving from mainstream to special education, and learning new skills such as Braille and mobility.

There was no comparable pathway of gender transformation, no support or access resources. Expressing the unspeakable would have undoubtedly resulted in bible-directed learning or electroconvulsive therapy.

There are implications in your journey, should you have a disability. Factors will vary between impairments. Without a doubt, mental health is common amongst those of us dealing with gender identity. With pressure to conform from family and wider society, challenges in getting timely and effective healthcare and financial consequences because of barriers to work, depression, stress and anxiety can take hold.

Blindness offered me different challenges from others taking our journey. Understanding how I presented visually was difficult, so taking advice was particularly important. That's not easy though when your friendship network is suddenly fractured and loneliness sweeps over everything you do. That means being bold and being prepared to take a few hits before you get it right.

Living as a woman isn't about being glamorous, although it could help. It isn't about clothes and make-up, but feeling good about yourself is what's important. You will want to 'pass' as a woman to avoid unwanted attention, but be minded to present without trying to be exceptional. My experience was to go orange when applying make-up, and the mirror didn't help, so I ditched it and have got on just fine without putting on a different face.

You have masses of information at hand, not least with online resources. Draw on the rich and diverse experience of those who have taken the extraordinary steps you are about to take. Research the options you are considering. With visual loss it wasn't possible for me to read printed information independently and there was no Internet in those days, so take advantage of the power information now has to offer.

Living a sheltered life at a Catholic boarding school that was segregated for visually impaired children proved to be remote from today's more liberated world. The notion of being gender different in that environment at that time was an unspeakable truth.

So I applied the proverbial saying that 'silence is golden', as saying nothing was wiser than speaking. As the poet Thomas Carlyle in *Sartor Resartus* (1831) wrote: 'Speech is silvern, Silence is golden; or as I might rather express it: Speech is of Time, Silence is of Eternity.'

Silence will afford protection for a while, but your inner self will ultimately need to find its voice. You have reached that critical moment for breaking that silence to be your true self. It takes a 'degree of audacity', but as my impossible dream became possible, you can believe too.

As you step through fear, you come to realise that things are different and your doubts don't come to fruition. People come alongside; you re-orientate and then find a new focus and momentum – in my case, to be Emily.

It was another disabled politician, Franklin Roosevelt, who said that 'the only thing we have to fear is fear itself'. Conquering fear is what I had to do when going on my journey – aligning to my female identity. That's now your endeavour – bringing your dream and reality into synergy.

We fear ridicule and mockery from the media. Whilst prejudice thrives amongst the tabloids, these aren't representative of a kinder and more tolerant country. Remember that newspapers only sell by whipping up controversy and they are no longer believed by large numbers of the public. What is far more important are your wellbeing and how your family and friendship networks get through this radical change. It will take re-orientation for all concerned. Trust has been shaken, like leaves falling from a tree, yet there will be another season of renewal if you work at re-building alliances.

So, sis, pause in the silence to think, press play to hear the symphony of voices and then sing to the tune that tells your unique story – live that dream with the pain and happiness it will engender. As the composer Meredith Monk puts it: 'That inner voice has both gentleness and clarity. So to get to authenticity, you really keep going down to the bone, to the honesty, and the inevitability of something.'

The inevitability is being you, being true, being authentic. So, sis, you can do it – go, go for it, girl!

Thank you kindly,

Emily

India Willoughby

....

Television personality India Willoughby made history as the first trans woman in the world to be a presenter on an all-female talk show when she was cast as a regular panellist on National Television Award-winning daytime TV show *Loose Women*, in 2016. Prior to this, and prior to transitioning, India worked as a newsreader on *ITV News* for ten years. Since coming out, she has used her platform to help educate the British public on trans issues.

....

Dear India (1981),

Yes, you – India. Don't bother looking over your shoulder for someone else. I'm talking to you, because India is your name. I know. Sounds a bit weird because everyone else calls you Jonathan, but nobody knows you like me. And in the future things are going to change. Quite dramatically. We both know what we're talking about. You're just not ready to tell everyone at the moment.

The first thing I need to tell you is that there is nothing more important than family. Nothing. When you tell them you-know-what in the future, cut them some slack. Be patient. It's going to be a bigger shock for them than it is to you. Tell them you love them. Particularly your mum. She's going to lose a son – which will be tough – but gain a daughter. Say that four-letter word spontaneously, whenever you feel like it, because life is simply too short.

You're going to be a dad. And a mum. In a manner of speaking. Your son will be a beautiful human being. Kind, clever and handsome. He's going to be your best pal as well as your kid. When he's six, he's going to play in a football match. Don't shout at him from the touchline because he's not playing well. Just because you were good at footy, doesn't mean that he has to be.

His talents lay elsewhere, and he's going to make you extremely proud.

Work-wise, you won't work in a clothes shop any more. You're going to be on the telly. First as a reporter, then as a newsreader. You'll love it – but a point will come when you have to walk away from your dream job. When this happens you will think your career is all over. It's not. You'll work as a Loose Woman. Not that sort of Loose Woman. Those two words have a very different meaning in 2017. You'll have three people come round to dine with you. Television cameras will be there, and the people at the table will give you points based on how much they enjoy what they eat. Do not under any circumstances make Spanish cheesecake using marmalade. Do a mousse, or something simple, and you will win.

You will escape from the body that never felt right and blossom. Don't pretend you don't know what I'm talking about. It's me you're talking to.

Most importantly, never give up. Even during some very dark, low times when you think life is simply not worth living, keep going, because you are protected by angels.

Be kind to people. Treat them as you expect to be treated.

Trust your gut instinct. Do not wear a high-collar black dress when you appear on a programme called *Celebrity Big Brother's Bit on the Side*. You will look like Morticia Addams.

Finally, the winning Euro-Lottery numbers for Friday, 21 April, 2017 are 02, 13, 16, 22, 49, 04 05.

Lots of love,

India (2017)

Şevval Kılıç

Şevval Kılıç is a prominent trans activist in Turkey and the founder of Istanbul Trans Pride. She is one of the founders of Women's Door, a non-governmental organisation that provides law and medical support for sex workers. She is also the founder of the Istanbul LGBTI+ Solidarity Association.

To my trans sisters,

My name is Şevval. I'm from Istanbul, Turkey, and I'm a 45-year-old anarco-queer/feminist non-binary trans woman. I was born a woman, but with a dick, and I never hated my dick – I just wanted to have a vagina more; it's as simple as that.

I don't want to give long, long advice to anyone but I have so much to share at the same time. I believe we live in a world controlled by patriarchy, but this part of the world especially is the Mecca of the patriarchy; for example, here in Turkey we love dick so much we worship it (of course by saying 'dick' I mean patriarch). I love dick but I have an issue with everything behind it politically. We built systems on it like family, religion, the binary system, etc., and every single trans individual shakes the main pillars of that rotten ideology by just being trans.

The world can be very cruel sometimes, because there are a lot of douche bags living in it. These douche bags sometimes are very much scared of people who don't follow the traditional norms, because then we become living proof that everything is possible, there are more than two genders and there are some really lucky people who see the other side of the rainbow – and it is beautiful.

There is no transphobia-free place in the world. Everywhere is the same, more or less, but even in that condition of the world I'm still so happy being me, having you, surrounded by awesome people.

Şevval Kılıç

Jordan Gray

....

Performer Jordan Gray came to the public's attention on BBC1's *The Voice* in 2016, making history as the show's first trans contestant (worldwide), winning over the hearts of the nation and making it all the way to the semi-finals on the show. Prior to appearing on the show, she toured and recorded under the pseudonym 'Tall Dark Friend'. After the show she released a music video for her hotly anticipated single 'Platinum', which is said to be the first mainstream music video to feature a romance between a transgender woman and a cisgender man. After ten years in the music industry she has made the leap from pop music to stand-up comedy.

....

To my trans sisters,

I'd like to geek out on you for a bit, if that's OK? I'm proper into science and evolutionary biology. A lot of my trans friends, for example, whom I deeply adore, are quite content to tell people that they are/were 'women trapped in men's bodies' or that they were 'supposed to be the other gender' or that their 'soul is female'. They have no desire to question any of that further, as though the fates have intervened in their lives and that's all they need to know.

I have to bite my tongue. If you're an anti-theistic, zero-spiritual social Darwinist like I am, your first few years after coming out may be spent nursing an existential angst. It's difficult to compartmentalise your desire to live an authentic life with the fact that the universe is essentially pointless. Don't worry about it. I've got you. Here's some sexy science for your ass.

In nature, there exists a phenomenon called 'sexual dimorphism' – the physical difference between the male and female of any given species. In humans, as with most mammals, it's not that big a deal. Naked and un-groomed, male and female humans look pretty much the same...especially compared to snakes or spiders. Think about chickens and roosters. Even cows and bulls.

But because our species evolved itself a sexy little thing called 'society'...and society favoured a patriarchy...we NEED that sexual dimorphism to distinguish the two genders and keep society churning. Otherwise everything falls apart – and there are a handful of people straddling the spike at the top of pyramid with a vested interest in things NOT falling apart. 100,000 years later, we have gender-specific garments and affectations to exaggerate a natural phenomenon into a false binary. Fuck all those non-binary and intersex people, right? Get back in yer box! Time is money!!

Unlike voles and porpoises, we are a self-aware species in a world that runs on arbitrary prejudice. Each of us plays a 'role' in a longstanding human game called 'gender'. There's another game called 'nationality' and another called 'class'. And people have a right proper sulk when they lose at either of those. Sometimes it gets nasty after a couple of wines and someone chucks something.

For those that depend on the game of 'gender' to give them a purpose, 'transgender' people are an affront to the rules. The existence of trans people seems to trivialise the achievements of the other players. Be patient with these players. They are fucking terrified that the world is crashing down around them.

For me, transitioning was a pragmatic decision, not an emotional one. I'm not a sociopath. I simply understand that (like Richard Dawkins will tell you re. the existence of God) merely 'believing' in something doesn't make it true. Sisters, we are not women because we 'feel' like it. What sort of an argument is that!? It's no wonder Germaine Greer wants to have a pop at us. The woman has done incredible things for feminism and here we are screaming, 'I do believe in fairies, I do, I do! I DO believe in fairies!' She's being a bit of a dick about it, but she's not totally 'wrong'.

Here is the salient piece of information you need. It's a bit of science + a bit of language theory + a bit of swearing...but stick with me for another couple of minutes and you'll have what you need to:

a) squash a TERF (trans-exclusionary radical feminist)
b) debate the validity of 'transgenderism'
c) justify grasping at meaning in a meaningless world.

So here's the crux: 'sex' and 'gender' are not the same thing: one is genetically assigned (sex) and will never change; the other is a construct (gender) and is malleable.

Are you still with me? We all KNOW that 'gender' and 'sexuality' are not the same thing. But society is yet to divorce 'gender' from 'sex' in common parlance. To be fair, it doesn't help that the word 'sex' has a dual meaning in English:

a) sexual intercourse
b) the arrangement of a person's chromosomes (XX, XY, etc.).

The English language fucks transgender people in the bum every day. I speak a tiny bit of Swedish and from what I can tell, that fucks us too...and, according to my research, so does Czech, German, French and Spanish. I got bored after that, but we can extrapolate from there.

The PROBLEM is: because we don't yet have 'sound-bitey' terms for 'XX' and 'XY', most people (including most of the medical profession) still refer to those chromosome arrangements as 'male' and 'female'. So when Germaine Greer says 'you can't change from male to female by putting on a frock', she's not being deliberately ignorant, she's just using English. Luckily, new words are invented every day and the words we already have change their meaning over time. Soon, if not sooner, the words 'male' and 'female' will refer exclusively to the construct of 'gender', and things should start to settle down for trans people. Clever, ain't I?

When you move from the 'male' sphere into the 'female' sphere, your sex doesn't change. This isn't *Jurassic Park II*. I will always be 'XY'. But if we engender the values of the 'sisterhood', the 'matriarchy', the 'sorority'...then we are women. It doesn't mean agreeing with everything other women say. It doesn't even mean being a feminist. 'Who you are' in life is not as important as 'What you do' with it.

The human willy is a funny little protrusion created by the presence of XY chromosomes. Inverting it doesn't change your genes to 'XX'. Just as painting yourself a different colour doesn't change your genetic lineage. That in mind, ask yourself how 'race' and 'nationality' are connected. This is an important bit:

One is genetically assigned (race) and will never change.
One is a construct (nationality) and is changeable.

Let's say you have a Jamaican lineage: your race is 'Jamaican'. Now let's say you were born and grew up in Jamaica too: your nationality is also 'Jamaican'. But if you move to another part of the world, imbibe yourself with the culture, prove your citizenship, you can change your nationality. Your race doesn't change. Your nationality does.

To put a more 'civil-rightsy' spin on the analogy, how long ago was it that 'race' and 'class' were unquestionably linked?

One is genetically assigned (race) and will never change.
One is a construct ('class') and is changeable.

People were just as uncomfortable seeing a black man in the 1950s go from 'lower class' to 'upper class' as they are today seeing somebody with XY chromosomes changing from a 'man' to a 'woman' before their very eyes. Being trans is an affront to many people's perception of reality. Do not attack them for this. You are revolutionary. You are beautiful (not that it matters). And you are real.

Jordan Gray

Brynn Tannehill

....

Veteran Brynn Tannehill was a key player inside the Pentagon, developing policy allowing transgender people to serve in the military. She was also a key author of the Department of Defense publication *Transgender Service in the US Military: An Implementation Handbook*. Brynn has been dubbed one of the great essayists of the transgender community and has written for the *New York Times*, *USA Today* and *The Advocate*, and has spoken at Harvard, Yale, the United States Naval Academy and the World Professional Association for Transgender Health. She was featured on the Trans 100 List in 2014.

....

To my (military) trans sisters,

Like everyone in the military, at some point I had to leave. Transitioning from military life to civilian is hard enough. Transitioning genders at the same time adds a degree of difficulty that even Greg Louganis would cringe at. I left active duty in 2008 after ten years in the service. I left the reserves in 2010 as Lieutenant Commander Bryan Tannehill. Less than two years later I was Brynn Tannehill, civilian defense contractor. Somehow, despite all the horror stories within the trans community, I managed to stay continuously employed, married, and maintaining most of the relationships that mattered most to me.

Some of this good fortune was due to sheer, dumb luck. The fact that I am still married is mostly due to the resilience, intelligence and adaptability of my spouse. Some of it is due to the work I put in to make sure I was making good decisions along the way. Good planning and good decisions had the most to do with why I am still employed. Since almost everyone in the military who gets out has to find a job at some point, tips on how to handle your transition at work seems to be the most generally applicable place to start.

Finding a spouse who will stick around for your transition is all on you.

Here are my thoughts and advice.

Know the battlespace

What does the corporate culture look like? What sort of rating does the company have on the Human Rights Campaign (HRC) Corporate Equality Index (CEI)? Does the company include gender identity in its corporate equal opportunity charter? What does the local office look like in terms of personality? It is entirely possible for a company to have a 100 percent rating with the HRC but be a terrible place to transition. If local leadership is hostile towards LGBT people, it does not matter what corporate policy is, transition is going to be rough at best. Conversely, if local leadership is supportive, even if corporate level policies are not, this makes transition much easier.

Know your rights

Just because your company doesn't include protections for gender identity, it doesn't mean that local or state ordinances won't provide them either. Even if local and state law don't provide protections, you still have rights via the courts and case law. The Equal Employment Opportunity Commission (EEOC) and the Justice Department in the United States have both established that being treated in a discriminatory fashion for being transgender is a form of sex discrimination, which is covered by the 1964 Civil Rights Act. Recent decisions such as *Glenn v Brumby*, *Macy v Holder*, *Smith v City of Salem*, and *Schroer v Library of Congress* have established via case law that discrimination based on gender expression violates both Title VII of the Civil Rights Act and the equal protection clause of the 14th Amendment.

Even if corporate policy and local laws do not protect you, you still have legal recourse via case law and EEOC policy.

Start saving now

Transition is very expensive. Most companies do not pay for sex reassignment surgery (SRS), and only a very small fraction pay for facial feminization surgery (FFS), laser, augmentations, etc. In a world where professional appearance may be everything, trying to transition without it may be a losing proposition if your goal is to stay employed in your field. Fortunately, the military is a good place to start building your savings, especially if you deploy frequently. Tax-free pay, combat pay, hazardous duty pay, and living in the field (or on the ship) all allow you to maximize income, and keep spending to a minimum if you are careful. My transition was basically paid for by a one-year unaccompanied tour in the sand box, during which I spent almost nothing, and lived on free food to the maximum extent practical.

So skip buying that new Mustang GT you wanted when you get back from deployment, and sock it away for future transition-related expenses. You will need it given FFS and SRS can run upwards of $50,000, and other transition-related items can add tens of thousands more.

Make sure the right people control your clearance

This one comes from personal experience. If at any point you change your name, and you are still in a position where you need a clearance, you will need to have that name change reflected in the Joint Personnel Adjudication System (JPAS). When you leave the military, make sure that your security officer, or base security, releases control of your clearance so your new employer can pick it up. Only the controlling authority can make the name change. If the Point of Contact (POC) information listed in JPAS is outdated, and you have long since moved on to the civilian side, getting your name changed in JPAS can be several months' worth of hassle. Worse, if you apply for a job in your new name, they might not be able to verify you have clearance.

Have a plan

At some point, you almost certainly have to come out to your employer. Hopefully, by the time you do, you will have evaluated the battlespace and gotten familiar with your rights, be they corporate, local, state, or case-law based. When you do go to your employer about your intent to transition, work through Human Resources (HR). When you tell your HR representative that you have been diagnosed with gender dysphoria and intend to transition, this is Health Insurance Portability and Accountability Act (HIPAA) protected information, and giving this information to anyone else requires your authorization. When you bring leadership in the company into the loop, do what you did in the military. When bringing your superior information about a problem, be ready to tell them exactly how you propose to address the issue. This can be timelines, training materials, suggestions on whom else in the company they can contact for further information (someone who has dealt with a similar situation), and ideas about how the transition should be handled with regards to the work environment.

When I came out to the Vice President (VP) in charge of our office (former Air Force Chief Master Sergeant), I had all of these things in writing, in a very nice-looking packet. He appreciated it, and that professionalism set the tone for the rest of the transition work done at my company.

Planning is everything, the plan is nothing

General Dwight Eisenhower said this almost 70 years ago, and it is still very true. No matter how well your plan for transition is, circumstances change. I had everything set up with my company to transition over a 14-month period. This included training schedules, surgery dates, meetings with Human Rights Campaign (HRC) people to develop training materials, checklists, Gantt charts, you name it. They worked great, right up until the Air Force cancelled the Global Hawk program. I lost all my research funding, and most of my team was being laid off. Suddenly, I had to use my planning and knowledge to cram my transition into three months of job hunting, surgery, name changes, legal document changes, covering my butt legally as I came out to a new potential employer, and a million other details.

The moral of the story was that because I had been so meticulous in laying the groundwork beforehand, when everything started to fall apart that knowledge and groundwork gave me the flexibility to accelerate everything by a factor of five.

It's not as bad as you think

Colin Powell wrote this as one of his 'rules'. I kept his list of rules on my desk for years, and it wasn't until I had finished transitioning that I realized he was right. Almost nothing about transition had been as bad as I expected. Not at home, not on the job, not in terms of legal protections, nor in terms of how many relationships I lost.

I didn't tell my (then) supervisor about being transgender until after I left the company. He was a retired Air Force Colonel, and I knew him to be a very conservative and religious person. I honestly expected a very negative reaction from him based on a host of profiling factors. After I left one employer as Bryan, and quietly started with another as Brynn, I finally told him what was going on in my life. His response surprised me. 'I don't give a ****. You're my friend. I'm just glad I don't have to sit through another one of those hour-long, guess-who's-coming-out-now diversity meetings. When you're recovered from surgery, let's have lunch.'

Yours in service,

Brynn Tannehill, LCDR USNR (ret)

Imma Asher

....

Imma Asher is a performance artist who has performed across America and Europe, danced with the Atlanta Ballet for three seasons, and been shot for SHOWstudio by Nick Knight. She has a BFA from Parsons and an MA from Central Saint Martins. Imma starred alongside trans model Hari Nef in the trailblazing Selfridges 'Agender' campaign, directed by Kathryn Ferguson, and co-stars in *Almost Saw the Sunshine*, a film directed by Leon Lopez.

....

To my trans sisters,

Take your time.

No! Really take your time.

You've probably just said 'Fuck off' and rolled your eyes as you've most likely already done your research and know everything about everything that you need and want out of your transition at this point.

Gigi Gorgeous, Laverne Cox, Janet Mock along with a stream of Internet babes have said it all.

Breathe.

Your chest is expanding and your nipples are extremely sensitive.

You're still looking for a job.

Delete Grindr (he's not there), along with expectations of self-presentation.

This is a proud moment.

Yes, you are a woman.

Yes, you will make it.

Yes, you deserve to be here.

Yes, it's extremely expensive.

Ease up in the contour and highlight, and stop using FaceTune.

See yourself.

Be proud.

Be strong.

Indulge in the transformation.

Read more.

Communicate and take ownership of you who you are.

You are amazing.

You are all things.

Put down the brow pencil.

Live.

And be happy.

You are everything.

You are a transwoman.

Imma

Juliet Jacques

....

Juliet Jacques is a British author and journalist. She documented her transition in her column in *The Guardian* in a series entitled 'A Transgender Journey', for which she was long-listed for the Orwell Prize for blogs in 2011. She went on to author *Trans: A Memoir*, for which she was runner-up in the Polari LGBT Literary Salon's First Book Award for 2016. Her work has also been featured in *New Statesman*, *The Washington Post* and *Time Out*. She was included on the *Independent on Sunday*'s prestigious Pink List of influential LGBT people in 2012, 2013, 2014 and 2015.

....

To my trans sisters,

I knew when I started that transition would complicate every aspect of my life: my body, most obviously, and my relationship with it, but also my relations with friends, family, colleagues, and the wider world. I hadn't quite anticipated how many people it would bring into my life – not just the medical professionals (providers of hormones and surgery, removers of facial hair and certain psychological burdens), but also people in the rich and varied trans communities. Those hadn't existed in the early 2000s, as I was struggling to work out exactly *what* my gender issue was, and couldn't find myself in Manchester's Canal Street, where older gay clubs were full of very masculine men and newer ones were full of straight women. But by the end of the decade, at least in Brighton, people *had* made those spaces, and I was so grateful to meet older trans people, especially trans women, who could guide me through the process in a way that forums and websites never quite could.

The women I met at the Clare Project – the drop-in support group in Brighton – gave me lots of tips, about the big things and the little. (I wish I'd got the advice not to buy large breast forms before I spent a hundred quid that I didn't really have; sure enough, as Raya told me, people were surprised to see my jutting chest when I started living as a woman, and the chest I ended up with after HRT wasn't as big.) I learned the importance of solidarity, and in particular, how difficult – and how important – it was not to let internalised transphobia keep me from forming bonds with trans women. That said, it was also good not to get *too* hung up on making trans friends but just to have friends in general. When I had a lot in common with someone, a shared trans history added another level; but one needs to remember that trans people are just as capable of having dreadful taste in music, becoming UKIP councillors or generally being dickheads as anyone else. (Even if one is prepared to be more forgiving due to the corrosive effects of transphobia, one cannot *always* blame that. Just when it's convenient.)

It's easy to fall into being a professional trans person, and it took me a long time to balance the need I felt to talk about gender with my other concerns – and with feeling like, and being treated as a rounded human being with diverse interests. Don't worry too much about fitting into ideas of what it means to be 'a woman' (be they your ideas, or other people's), and definitely don't suppress any parts of your personality for that reason. It will strike your friends as strange, and do far more to make you feel inauthentic than any of those boring clickbait articles where some old school feminist decries trans identity. (One piece of advice: get into media commissioning so you have the power to decline such tired old tropes.)

Seriously, though – be yourself. Transition will change the way that people respond to you in ways that you can't control, and so it *will* change you, of course – for the better, in many ways, despite all the difficulties. Don't expect it to be a panacea for everything – I had problems with depression and anxiety before I began the process, and still have them now – and don't feel that you can't express any struggles to anyone. This has never been easy, and there's no shame in finding it tough: you can't stand up to transphobia in every second of your life, no matter how much you do, and putting pressure on yourself won't be good for you. Find as much support and community as you need, keep some time and space for yourself, and trust yourself – nobody begins this process lightly, after all.

Juliet Jacques

Gogo Graham

·····························

Gogo Graham is a fashion designer from New York who has showcased at New York Fashion Week and been featured in many publications, including *Dazed and Confused*, *i-D* and *Vogue*. She makes custom clothing exclusively for trans women, and uses her collections to address issues such as trans violence. *Dazed and Confused* magazine named her as one of New York Fashion Week's breakout designers after she showcased her collection with an all-trans line-up.

·····························

To my trans sisters,

Find shoes in which you feel able to run. Make sure they fit properly.

Gogo Graham

Robyn Alice McCutcheon

....

Robyn Alice McCutcheon is a foreign service officer with the US Department of State and a past president of GLIFAA, the association representing LGBT+ employees of the State Department, USAID, and other foreign affairs agencies. Serving currently in Central Asia, she has also served as a diplomat at US embassies in Moscow, Bucharest and Washington, DC. Prior to this, she worked at NASA on missions such as the Hubble Space Telescope and has published work on the history of Soviet science.

....

Dear Sis,

August 1975. It's summer in Virginia, hot and humid. There's a knock at my door, and I freeze. I have few friends, and most of them have left for the summer. I'm sweating...and not only from the heat. I don't move a muscle, don't make a sound, scarcely breathe. My double life is a secret one. I'm sick, diseased. No one else in the world is like me. To be disclosed will bring shame on me, shame on my family. There will be no future. I'll spend my life medicated in institutions. The knock repeats, and still I hold my breath. A third time. A fourth. Then I hear footsteps walking away and breathe a sigh of relief.

Could that have been you, soul sister, come back in time to tell me that there is a future, to tell me it does get better?

April 2016. I first notice you on your knees looking at my collection of vinyl records, a Joni Mitchell album in your hands. 'Can we play this one?' Of course we can. I help you put the needle down gently, and the sounds of 'Both Sides Now' and 'The Circle Game' fill my apartment on the Central Asian steppe at a latitude approximating the northern tip of Newfoundland.

I was hosting a welcome dinner. The next day we would open a roundtable on transgender rights, the first of its kind seen in this country. I was one of the organizers, and soon my attention was taken by other guests. Even Jamison Green from the World Professional Association for Transgender Health had come. Such is the life of a US foreign service officer, a diplomat, who 'does it all,' giving attention to all to the depth that time and issues allow.

But I didn't forget you. Weeks later I was in your city. We had late evening coffee and cheesecake. Only 18, you had been kicked out of your school that year because of who you are. Surely I could get you into another?

Over the months I came to know you better. Never had I met someone who had the same taste in music as I do. It's more than 'the same'. Our tastes are identical. How is it that you know American singer-songwriters of the 1960s and '70s better than I do? How could this be when you live on the other side of the world, where you had to learn English on your own? Just listening to the music you love brings me back to my own past and the chance I had but let get away. Surely such things happen only in 'The Twilight Zone?'

I never opened that door in 1975. I hid hard in the closet, doing all I could 'to make this go away'. I used drugs, but my drug of choice was the one most acceptable to society: work. I threw myself into it to drown out the white noise of my life.

The decades to come saw me succeed in the eyes of the world. I worked on NASA missions and spent many years in the Hubble Space Telescope project, but that was not enough. I threw myself equally hard into Russian history as an escape. I lived the lives of Soviet astronomers and their families in the 1930s, reading their letters in dusty archives and in family libraries. Repressed for no good reason, many of them were executed or died in the Gulag. Living their lives and writing about them for the world, I didn't have to face my own. 'Welcome, Repression Workshop!' proclaimed the hotel sign at a conference where I spoke in Austin, Texas, in 1986. 'If they only knew,' I silently thought to myself. In 1989 a respected historian came up to me after I had spoken at a conference and poked his finger in my chest. 'I want to know what makes you tick,' he said. I only answered him honestly some 25 years later.

To the world I was a NASA professional, an 'attitude analyst', a recipient of awards and an academic with published research and conference papers. But inside I was a disaster. I had married, thinking this is what society expected. When she found out the truth, my spouse never forgave me. We were little better than co-parents to our one child, the miracle of a troubled marriage. 1990 saw me spend a week in a psychiatric ward, the first time I sat with a psychiatrist. I ended up at Johns Hopkins' Sexual Behavior Unit, the domain of the now debunked anti-trans crusader Paul McHugh. My brief attempt to be myself failed in 1990, just as it had in 1975. The story repeated in 2000 with another visit to Hopkins. I changed careers, moving from the engineering of NASA to the diplomatic craft of the US State Department. Only in 2010–11 did the miracle finally happen. After three failed transition attempts, the fourth succeeded, just as I had concluded I would go to my grave as I was.

In this, now the sixth decade of my life, I am living a miracle. You have become my much younger soul sister. I'd like to think of myself as your surrogate Mom, but I've met your Mom and know I could not replace someone so wonderful and supportive. Still, forgive me if I have feelings that can only be described as maternal.

April 2017. You are poised for a new adventure, about to become what in my day we would have called a co-ed at a college in my own country. I know you're scared. Change is hard even when it's change for the good. As your older soul sister, I can assure you that succeeding in college is the easy part. You've accepted yourself and gotten those who are dearest to you to accept you. That was the hard part. You will miss your Mom and close friends over the coming months, but they will wait for you and cheer you on. So will I. You are wise beyond your years, far wiser than I was in that decade long ago.

August 1975. Could that have been you at my door, soul sister, come back through the space–time continuum to give me hope? In my heart I know it was you. You came back to tell me not to be afraid, to trust myself that no matter what society would throw at me, I would live to be myself. If you come again, and that moment repeats, don't walk away. Break down the door if you must. Take me by the hand and walk me out into the world. I will show you the stars, and you will teach me to be me right then and there while my entire life awaits. Together we will walk out into a hot and humid University of Virginia evening and sit on The Lawn under a full moon, listening as someone strums a guitar and sings the songs we both love while they're still fresh and new.

Your loving soul sister,

Robyn Alice

Andrea James

....

Andrea James is a writer, producer and activist. In 1996, during the Internet's infancy, she created the hugely popular and important 'Transsexual Road Map', a resource website for transgender people, which helped a generation to transition efficiently. She also created a plethora of instructional videos for trans women to support them through transition, such as *Finding Your Female Voice*. Andrea produced and performed in the first all-transgender cast of *The Vagina Monologues* in 2004, directed *Alec Mapa: Baby Daddy*, and consulted on the Academy Award-nominated feature film *TransAmerica*, coaching Felicity Huffman to her Golden Globe win.

....

To my trans sisters,

It's been decades now, and I'm still in transition.

We're constantly in transition, though most of us rarely think about the many ways we're changing minute by minute. Each day we move through the world, and we hurtle through time. Our experiences change us, and each day is an opportunity to gain new insight and wisdom.

A gender transition is expensive, stressful and draining, yet you have the ability to reach your goals through realistic expectations and self-acceptance. How many people in the world will ever be able to say they accomplished something that challenging? How many people can say they realized their childhood dreams? You've been given a great gift. Please put it to good use.

If we're open and perceptive to them, we can glean great insights from a gender transition. The greatest insight? Transition can liberate you from fear. As much as we might hope and dream and plan, transition is ultimately a leap of faith, an act of courage. It's never easy, and it's never over. As I write this, many years have passed since my own transition, and I continue to learn more about myself each day. I never take my good fortune for granted, and I have worked hard to help others have an easier time than I did, because I was in a position to do so. If you give of yourself without expecting anything in return, your gift will come back to you in all sorts of surprising and unexpected ways.

Many of us have a sense of feeling lost after transition, similar to scaling a difficult mountain, getting to the top, and looking out over the breathtaking vista of everywhere else you could go. As the exhilaration and awe wear off, at some point you must leave that mountain top in order to get on to the next challenge.

The spectacular view doesn't begin at the top of the mountain. You must find joy in the difficult journey itself, at each step. You must look up and around now and then, to marvel at how far you've already come. So many of us will miss the incredible experiences along the way. We often get so caught up in the 'during' of transition, that we do not marvel at the joys each day can bring. Some even get so exhausted and depleted from the transition process, that they don't seek out a new ambitious challenge after transition. That is perhaps the greatest tragedy that can befall you after transition.

My therapist once told me, 'There's never a happy ending to an unhappy journey.' Don't get so focused on your transition goals and outcome that you defer other dreams.

If you can transition, you can do almost anything else about which you feel that passionately. You have to be very honest about what else you want in life, though. I made the difficult decision to leave graduate school, despite getting into the PhD program, because I didn't want to spend my life around the kinds of people I'd met in grad school. I got out of advertising because I just did it to make money for transition. Now I create whatever I want and only work with good friends.

What is most important to you? Love? Privacy? Fame? Family? Respect? Health? Solitude? Faith? Stability? Chaos? Only you can answer via deep introspection. Your answer may change over time, too, so ask yourself often.

The best thing you can do after transition is unplug from the trans scene for a bit and get a fresh perspective. What else do you feel as strongly about as your gender identity? How else would you like to move through the world? What other communities are important to you?

What kind of work would you do if money were not an issue? Then why are you not doing that work? Do what you love and do it well. The money will come, and you will be happier.

How could your social life be different? It's critical to get out of your comfort zone and try new things. It will really help change your focus.

Think about what challenges make you happy in life. If you accept challenges – large and small – each day and have fun while working on them, there's almost nothing you can't do.

You're already on the path to accomplishing something extraordinary. Now it's time to accomplish something else extraordinary!

Andrea James

Marci Bowers

....

Dr. Marci Bowers, MD, is a pioneering gynaecology surgeon, best known for her sex reassignment work. She is considered to be an innovator in her field and is also notably the first trans woman to perform this surgery. She has appeared as a guest on *The Oprah Winfrey Show* and *The Tyra Banks Show* and been the subject of numerous documentaries. Marci is also well known for, and considered to be an international authority on, clitoral reconstruction for women who have suffered female genital mutilation (FGM). She is one of the few surgeons in the world performing functional FGM reversal and does this at no cost to patients.

....

To my trans sisters,

Gender transition is the most magical, terrifying, challenging, exciting, frustrating, disappointing, wonderful direction your life will ever take. It is a delicate path. Tread lightly, like walking on lily pads. Be careful. Most importantly, learn to live by intuition. Your life greatly impacts those around you. Living with sensitivity does not come easily for many. Incorporation of this attitude will generally serve you well.

The decision

To be or not to be, that is the question. For most, it is pretty easy. It is something we have fought most of our lives, trying to be that square peg in the round hole. It hasn't worked. Something needs to change. I tried at age 19 but I couldn't manage it at the time and it took me another 19 years to try again. But, when I did, there was little to slow me down. Don't rush! Transition is like climbing a ladder. Stop along the way and enjoy the view. Transition is as close to a cliché spiritual path as there is in the human experience. Most of my truly miraculous moments happened while 'in the middle', before completing the process surgically. Enjoy that time in the middle and make it work for you.

Coming out

There is an overwhelming temptation to come out before you are really 'ready for prime time'. Do your homework. Make it easier (for you and for others) by clearing hair and growing hair, adopting a personal style that works, appearing in public, and, above all, preparing others. That means coming out. It can be terrifying. Somehow, I managed to do it wrong on most occasions. For example, wearing a dress and make-up to a pharmaceutical dinner with my professional practice partner – talk about an awkward dinner conversation! Or the other time with my neighbor/best friend, whom I asked to meet for 'something important' – for me, it was about transition; but for my friend, who had been through a series of frustrating infertility treatments and was seeking adoption, saw my invitation as a suggestion that I, as a practicing obstetrician/gynecologist, had found an adoption candidate. Seeing me in a dress was a crushing moment for her on two fronts. That moment permanently damaged our friendship and it has never been the same. People don't see transition coming, no matter how feminine your male persona may already be. Just remember, it's not always about you! There just never is a perfect time to announce a gender change. I came out to my three kids, aged one, four, and five, by attending dinner at a Chinese restaurant in Penticton, British Colombia, in drag. Now THAT was fun! Why? Because, now that we can all look back, the situation was hilarious. It made the movie, *A Christmas Story*, look like a funeral in comparison. If you can find humor in any of this, survival is possible.

Jewelry

When you are finished dressing, subtract one piece of jewelry. Remember, you aren't leaving your apartment to meet RuPaul.

Workplace

You are transitioning to a happier place, hopefully. When you arrive for work as the person you see yourself to be, let that feeling show. Smile. Walk proudly. Hold your head high. Sure, you will have some detractors who will try to drag you into a negative place, but there will also be many others who affirm you in ways never imagined. And don't forget to laugh. When you laugh, the world will laugh with you. But, no matter how difficult, *stay in your job!* Unless you are hoping to retire, do not let harassment get to you. Do not voluntarily leave, above all, without a fight. You were good enough before transition. You are surely a better, happier employee after transition.

Rejection

Transition is difficult. It will challenge notions of who you are and how others see you. Hopefully, you were a nice person BC (Before Change – yeah, I came up with that). If not, transition is a chance to re-boot your personality! Make the most of it. Show that kindness, that softness, the sweetness that is really you. But don't get cloyingly sweet. Be yourself but let it go! There will be many who see the new you and others who will not be open. It's OK – for every loss, there is always more than one gain. Support will come from people you might not expect to give it. Even less predictable is the loss you will experience from those you thought were friends. It is highly unpredictable, but remember, it is not about you. So let it go and experience something new.

I could go on and on but for now, have fun.

Marci

Michelle Hendley

....

Award-winning actress Michelle Hendley is best known for playing the lead role of Ricky in *Boy Meets Girl*, a groundbreaking film that boldly features a love story between a cisgender boy and a transgender girl played by actors of the respective gender identities. Director Eric Schaeffer discovered Michelle on YouTube, where she was documenting her transition, and though she had no prior acting experience she went on to win the award for best actress at the FilmOut Festival for her role in the film.

....

To my trans sisters,

I think prior to our transitions we express our internalized femininity in different ways. For me it was through drawing, comic books and video games. These mediums allowed me to visualize myself as the female heroes and avatars I loved so much. My entire youth was focused on honing my art, living through imagination and aspiring to make my passion for the female form a possible profession as an animator and character designer. I did not, however, anticipate the dramatic and all-consuming effect gender transition would have over my life. It was no longer satisfactory to internalize Wonder Woman, because I wanted to *be* Wonder Woman. I eventually lost my will to draw heroines and write stories, and I put all of my attention into designing my own image.

Admittedly, after popping that first little blue pill, my entire transition became a fixated obsession with attaining an aesthetic. I wanted bawdy. I wanted to be fishy, cunt, and not just passable but beautiful. I was hellbent on procedures and surgeries, exercising, perfecting my hormone dosage and establishing a wardrobe that reflected my new-found womanhood. The first few years of my twenties were such a constant laser focus on beauty and physicality that I ended up at beauty school and became a licensed cosmetologist. I was absolutely, selfishly and unapologetically dedicated to taking ownership of a body I had resented for so many years.

Once the smoke cleared, so to speak, I was left with a body I could accept and one very big question: *Who is Michelle?* The longer I thought about it, the further I seemed to get from the answer. *Who is this woman I have become? What are her aspirations? Her passions?* I imagined a great blank slate with my name at the top, and realized that I had completely lost sight of my identity as anything more than a transgender woman. It was as though I had drawn out the perfect super-heroine but neglected to establish her back story and character. I once called myself an artist and a gamer, someone who always carried a sketchbook and the latest issue of a comic, but these things no longer applied to me. It is a daunting thing to not know yourself, despite spending countless hours and days over-analyzing every detail of your gender and body. I felt lost, empty and once again desperate to know myself.

It is important to remember that every person on this little blue planet is in a state of flux and change. Every day we, trans and cis folk alike, are growing, learning and adjusting to the world around us. In much the same way we trans women are not who we were before transition, I think non-trans people are not who they were ten, twenty, or even just five, years ago. We are all given the space and agency to evolve at any point we choose, and it was this realization that helped me to answer that big question about my identity. I may not have a definite answer to who I am or even who I want to be, but I am that much closer to knowing every single day.

The day and the absolute second we come to recognize and embrace our truth is the very moment that we are allowed to start ourselves anew. It is a release and a freedom from a life that we never really asked to live in the first place, and our first step toward living authentically. I congratulate you and every trans woman who is able to boldly face herself, perceived flaws and all, and see that she is absolutely worth the love, care and compassion that she deserves. So please, for everything you are, let transition be a celebration of the person you never thought you could be, because in this moment you are that person.

All my love and admiration,

Michelle

Ellie Krug

....

Ellie Krug is an American lawyer, writer and activist. In 2016, *Advocate* magazine named her as one of the '25 Legal Advocates Fighting for Trans Rights'. In 2009, while she was an Iowa civil trial attorney with 100+ trials to her name, she transitioned from male to female, becoming one of the few attorneys nationally to try jury cases in both genders. She has also served as Executive Director of Call for Justice, LLC, a Minneapolis legal non-profit organisation, which was given an American Bar Association award for innovatively increasing legal access. Ellie recently authored a memoir, *Getting to Ellen: A Memoir about Love, Honesty and Gender Change*.

....

To my trans sisters,

There are a million things that I could say to you, but I'll settle with this: 'There is no such thing as a Human Owner's Manual.'

It's absolutely true. We have no big book filled with answers that we might resort to in times of self-doubt or fear or hurt. Because of this, we're often left to figure things out through our own fragile devices. I call it 'reading tea leaves' – if tonight's moon is full and the North Star extra bright, and tomorrow's temperature won't exceed 43 degrees at the airport, then for sure I will make that big decision...

If you're transgender, not having a Human Owner's Manual has particular significance. After all, most of us have no idea of how to handle gender dysphoria (the incongruity between brain and body) or how to deal with those who refuse to accept us as our 'true' (brain-unified-with-body) selves.

It's the latter quandary that I've been thinking about of late, largely because of a recent audience member's question, to wit: 'What advice do you have for a transgender person who's lost people in their life?'

We trans humans commonly lose people. I can go to any gathering of transgender folks and simply ask, 'Who have you lost?' and everyone will know that the question isn't about loved ones or friends who have died.

Rather, the common understanding would be this: who among the trans person's family members, friends or work colleagues has chosen not to recognize that person for whom they truly are? We're talking about people who mistakenly believe that coming out as trans or transitioning genders is a choice. Often the response is: 'You've made a choice about being you and now I'm going to choose not to accept that.'

The common modality is that those who refuse to accept us simply stop communicating, hence they become 'lost'. When this happens, it hurts. A lot.

Some of you reading this will have parents or grandparents or siblings who've turned their backs. Some will have lost an adult child or a best friend. Always, it's someone close, a human who mattered and whose rejection now – at this critical time your life – is particularly difficult to accept or handle.

In fact, being rejected by these people just sucks. Sorry to be so blunt (and un-feminine-like), but it's true. When I transitioned in 2009, I lost many people – my sister, my best friend in my hometown and an across-the-street neighbor, who also happened to be a federal magistrate (and as a trial lawyer who regularly appeared in federal court, that was particularly problematic).

Most importantly, I lost the light of my life, my oldest daughter (who was then in her late teens). We didn't see each other for two-and-a-half years, and went months without talking by phone. Email and Facebook communications were non-existent.

Losing my daughter broke my heart. I can't even begin to count the tears or describe the feeling of desperation.

And then, with a great deal of work on both our parts, as well as yeoman-degree assistance from several therapists, my daughter came back to me. So much so, she's now 'pronoun proper' and perfectly accepting. It is, as I once wrote, the greatest gift I could ever ask for.

So, what's my advice for you, relative to the people you've lost?

As I see it, you have two choices. One choice is to react back just as you've been reacted to – because the other person's closed their heart to you, you can reciprocate by closing yours to them. I call this 'tit for tat hurt' – you've hurt me, so I'll hurt you back. While this helps to stem bleeding of the heart (albeit, the wound never closes entirely), I don't see this as a good strategy for one important reason: people change. Indeed, with more and more humans coming out as transgender, society as a whole is quickly becoming more accepting of trans folk. This means that people whom we've lost might reconsider their decision to shut us out.

Rather than closing your heart, I recommend keeping it open. For sure, that's far more work and hurt since the wound and vulnerability remain. Yet, staying open – in effect keeping the door to reconciliation unlatched – makes it easier for the other person to come back. This is the epitome of compassion for another human: you're recognizing that they too, lack a Human

Owner's Manual and are willing to help them make their way back to you.

I can attest that the open heart strategy works. Apart from my daughter, other people I had lost have now come back (including my sister). It sure stank while they were gone, but in the end, I have these people in my life again, accepting me. For that, I am extremely grateful. I'm glad that the tea leaves told me to keep my heart open.

Living authentically – being true to yourself – doesn't come cheaply or easily. For that reason, many people don't transition genders; instead, they stay hidden, hurting and depressed, and not knowing the taste of authenticity. For those people, I feel genuine sorrow.

For you who have come out, congratulations! Remember that life is ever-changing.

And so are people.

Ellie

Pauline Park

....

Pauline Park, PhD, is Chair of the New York Association for Gender Rights Advocacy (NYAGRA). She led the campaign for the transgender rights law enacted by the New York City Council in 2002 and also participated in the working group convened by the New York City Commission on Human Rights that drafted guidelines for implementation of the statute. She was a member of the steering committee that led the campaign for enactment of the Dignity for All Students Act (DASA) and negotiated inclusion of gender identity and expression in that legislation, the first transgender-inclusive legislation enacted by the New York state legislation when it was signed into law in 2011. She was named one of the '50 Transgender Icons' and ranked one of 'The Most Influential LGBT Asian Icons' by the *Huffington Post*.

....

To my trans sisters,

I've been coordinator of the transgender support group at Queens Pride House for six years now and I've been doing lesbian, gay, bisexual and transgender (LGBT) community activism for 23 years. I've lived my entire adult life as an openly non-heteronormatively identified person, first coming out as gay when I turned 18 and then as transgendered when I was 36. Over the course of many years I've known thousands of transgendered people, and the one piece of advice I would offer to anyone is to listen to the stories of those who have gone before one and then chart one's own path. The mainstream media focus almost obsessively on what I call the 'classic transsexual transition narrative', which is a linear movement from diagnosis to hormones, with sex reassignment surgery as the end point of the transition. While some do pursue this path, far more pursue a different path, some pursuing non-linear transitions, and many choosing not to do hormones and/or surgery. As I like to say, there are as many different ways of being transgendered and of transitioning as there are transgendered people. Be open to information, suggestions and advice from others and join a support group if you think it would be helpful, but find your own path and don't allow peer pressure to pressure you into following someone else's. Above all, heed the advice Polonius gave to Laertes: 'To thine own self be true.'

Pauline Park

Rhyannon Styles

....

Journalist and author Rhyannon Styles is best known for her popular column in *Elle* magazine, 'The New Girl', where she documents her transition and discusses trans issues. She recently authored a memoir, *The New Girl: A Trans Girl Tells It Like It Is*, for Headline. Rhyannon is also a performance artist, with highlights of her performance career including shows at the Guggenheim Museum in New York and the Barbican in London, and performing with Kylie Minogue on ITV. She was featured on the *Independent on Sunday*'s Rainbow List under 'ones to watch' and made a cameo appearance in the BBC 2 drama *Boy Meets Girl*.

....

To my trans sisters,

If you're about to embark upon the journey to reveal the true you, then fasten your seatbelt, as you're in for a bumpy ride. But don't worry, here are some of my tools to help YOU blossom.

Rhyannon Styles' Transitioning Tool Kit

MUSIC — MAKE A PLAYLIST OF YOUR FAVOURITE SONGS
Choose the songs that make you smile, laugh, dance and be silly. If you love singing along to your favourite pop star in the mirror,

wishing you could be them, then do it. Do that every single day. You have my guarantee that whenever you feel frustrated that your hair isn't growing quick enough, once you've belted out your favourite song on repeat, you'll forget all about it.

FRIENDS — SPEND QUALITY TIME WITH YOUR BFS

Invite your friends out to lunch or the cinema to watch the latest horror film. Take long walks and spontaneous shopping trips. Spend as much time with them as you possibly can. Your friends are your main support network, and you'll definitely need a hug every now and again. It's important that you don't neglect your friendships. It's not just YOU who is transitioning; your friends need time to adjust too.

MONEY — START SAVING YOUR PENNIES

There's nothing more delicious than making yourself feel like YOU, trust me. Legally changing your name, buying new clothes and laser hair removal all costs money. So start a transition fund and treat yourself. It's time to invest in YOU.

PATIENCE — IS YOUR SECOND BEST FRIEND

Believe it or not, a transition can't happen overnight. You can't flick a switch and suddenly expect to be the person you've always dreamed of. Unfortunately, it doesn't happen like that. To transition is to change your life, the lives of those around you and your place in society. It's a slow process, for good reason. Remember to breathe.

LOVE — LEARN TO CULTIVATE THAT FEELING!

It all starts with YOU, remember that. Sometimes the world will seem like it's against you, with people saying things that may upset you. During the turbulence make sure you look after your needs. Nurture the love you feel inside yourself. This is a journey of self-love, self-care and self-acceptance.

Stand up, stand out, be bold and be proud. Most importantly, be YOU.

Love,

Rhyannon

Lana Pillay

....

Lana Pillay is a British pop, TV and film star best known for appearing in Channel 4's groundbreaking *The Comic Strip Presents*, and as the protagonist in the film *Eat the Rich* alongside Paul McCartney, Jennifer Saunders and Dawn French. As a disco diva she ruled the dance floor in the mid-1980s with the disco classic 'Pistol in my Pocket', and in the 1990s she was featured on the Gary Clail smash hit 'Human Nature', appearing twice on BBC's *Top of the Pops*, and for eight consecutive weeks on MTV's *Chart Show*.

....

To my trans sisters,

I would never, ever refer to myself as transsexual, as an agender, gender-fluid person (even though I need no box). Spiritually and personally I do not believe in gender, anybody's gender. I was always demisex, meaning I am someone who doesn't feel or fully identify with their assigned gender but doesn't have a vehement enough dysmorphia to associate with the other. I understand gender from an optic of being an essentialist social CON-struct and an existentialist truth. However, for many of us there is no truth in it whatsoever – tits and fanny do not a woman make, nor cock and balls a man make. These instruments are only external configurations of the organs used for reproduction (however, the reproductive system or genital system of sex organs do not work for everybody, for the many non-living substances such as fluids, hormones and pheromones remain non-living in many cases and refuse to play their important roles as accessories to reproduction or for sexual pleasures, so screw those parochial-minded types that think in their delusional and ill-informed states that they have a handle on it, the bloody know-it-alls) and God knows I've flattened plenty of grass in me time after dark, behind a privet hedge. Still do! Well not so much behind a bush these days as inconsiderate types don't pick up after their dogs, innit, haha!

I wasn't quite happy to accept a transsexual identity just for the sake of respectability politics. Bollocks to the heteroid dominant usuality and its fear of taking a deeper trip within its own dysfunction and broadening its understanding of the human condition. Seems to be far more satisfied with its hetero wars that normalize mass-destruction and over-populating the planet with unwanted, unloved, starving, poverty-stricken, abused children and all the damaging pathology that is horribly hardwired into the frontal cortex of those poor things. So don't make me wet my Coco de Mer. After all, tis I that has had to tolerate them all my life and not the other way round, but in the gender-bending climate of 1980s London and against the prism of Thatcher's cruel, racist LGBTQ-phobic right-wing England I experienced a lot of attention, negative and positive, for being a high-profile, blazing, brown transsexual (or drag queen with a great pair of hooters as perceived by society's inadequates). It was a bitter-sweet life. Being non-white, much of the oppression levelled at me was more pronounced and it came from all sides and from all levels: black, white and whatever!!! It was tough and I still bear some of the mental scars and anger of it all. It has not dissipated as much as I'd like, so I've just pushed it around to places where it doesn't hurt me as much, as you never stop unpacking the trunk. I hastily add that I have only ever represented myself. I don't speak for anyone else except for those I'm on the same page with, and outside of my audiences I am not a fan of half my species – the inhuman race.

However, after coming off hormone treatment during the filming of *Eat the Rich* with *The Comic Strip Presents*, and suffering a semi-nervous breakdown (a very depressive, debilitating, dark period), I came to realize that gender is a myth and that it doesn't really exist for any of us – for me, the main issue is being in the body but not of it, regardless of the defence folk put up regarding chromosomes and biological facts (a thread-like structure of nucleic acids and protein found in the nucleus of most living cells carrying the information in the form of genes...and, NO!, wearing Levis does not maketh the man or lumberjack Jack, innit). We all know that gender or the idea of gender resides in the mind and not between our legs, but even Professors Richard Dawkins and Stephen Hawkins have no idea where thought comes from – they say they think it comes from the mind, but being born of the primary feminine (the divine feminine, that is, babes!) in a male-based system, for me I see taking hormones much the same as using software to produce the aesthetic I like and am very comfortable with and not to create a schism between thoughts and feelings within the neural pathways. It's a bloody shame they can produce a lot of adipose tissue on the body though, but then you just have to walk and weight-lift more and cut out the bad carbs – you know, chips, crisps, cakes, biscuits...and girl, forget bread...the whiter the bread, the sooner yo is dead!

Too many people I see these days live in a delusional state. We have all kinds of folk professing 'I'm trans!' and becoming the dupes of their own existence. Actually, what do you mean by declaring 'I'm trans'? Maybe you are just jumping on a current trendy bandwagon, using it as a shock tactic like some deep-seated primal scream for attention. I've found that a lot of unself-examined people do! I'm not saying that gender isn't something to be played with, but when certain individuals I meet say they want gender reassignment, as a sentient and all-knowing being I have to suggest other alternatives. I often advise them to do go see a gender psychologist first, get some hormones, laser treatment, feminize, get some boobs (they are only signifiers of something, after all), work that for a while, explore whether your desperation and desire for reassignment is so compelling, as I'm not convinced of their compulsion being that of a genuine transsexual.

And just to dovetail all of this, I have to state that I don't want society to treat me as and pretend that I'm a natal female woman as that is not my experience. I have arrived at my earthbound gender identity led by the critical mass and prefer female gender pronouns as male ones are almost as alien and surreal to me as this planet I reside on and this mental matrix of life I experience on this spinning rock in space. It is society that demands we fit in the box on this front, but then I've never fitted in and never want to. In fact, the terminology for somebody like me has not been touched upon yet. I believe gender dysphoria is a dysfunction of a dysfunctional global heterosexual dominant usuality that purports to be normative – a schism of itself that's a load of old bollocks in my opinion, innit. And I do know that being male or female is not gender behaviour, but is human behaviour. There is no such thing as being a real woman, or a real man, and buying into a patriarchal

CON-struct of being a woman makes us as misogynistic as the outmoded model it's sold upon. I think by the very nature of this word and the arduous struggle, 'transgenderism' affirms and reaffirms the gender binary. Individuals tend to move from one gender to another, when indeed there is a broad spectrum of gender underlining them. On the one hand, we've got a group of people that are terrorized and persecuted for their gender, and on the other hand we have the very existence of this group feeding back into the societal problem. That's not to say I want to shut trans individuals out of the discussion, negate or invalidate what they face – I've known first-hand, based on empirical evidence, what ostracism, flak, ridicule and violence feels like and how this impacts a person to the very core of our being even in casual conversation. Trans or not, or whatever identity an individual chooses on that broad spectrum of self-identities, I maintain that gender, just like religion, is an invention CON-structed to keep us all separated and at war with each other in order to negate respect for the human condition. Gender is not real, not mine, not yours, not Germaine Greer's, not Jenni Murray's, not Caitlyn Jenner's, not anybody's – it's all a scam used to keep us at loggerheads with one another, to subjugate and arrest our progress in the fleeting time we are here on this planet and to use some of us that don't, can't, and won't fit or conform to CON-ventional norms as a punch-bag for its own neurosis. It would be naive of anybody not to notice some differences, but I believe these gender difference stereotypes are societal and ingrained in us.

And to finish off, I say that only neurotics genderize and demean, so play with gender, apparel and belief. Examine deeper feelings and imagery. Live the life that's best for you, live a wonderful self-fulfilling life too and stand for no shit. You already arrived in this life fully formed. Nobody is worth more points than you, there is no hierarchy of birth class, creed, colour, status, sexual orientation or gender – although I have found many trans people to be highly intelligent and generous of spirit, but then we've trod a rockier path in some ways, innit! And regardless of the inordinate and unhealthy inadequates out there and their weird secret obsession with what yo got between yo legs or shoved on yo chest – fuck all these failed humans, these earthbound misfits, perverts and inverts. And finally, always try do whatever good you can, from wherever you are, with whatever you've got, because when it all boils down to it, at the end of the day, there are only two types of people in this world: they are either a C*NT OR THEY ARE NOT!... In my experience, based on empirical evidence.

Lana Pillay

Shon Faye

....

Broadcaster and stand-up comic Shon Faye is best known for her viral social media video series, *Shon This Way*, where she discusses LGBTQ issues. She has been featured in films for the Tate and Channel 4, and has also appeared on BBC *Newsnight* and BBC 3's *Queer Britain*. Shon is a columnist for *Dazed*, a regular contributor for *Novara Media* and has also written for publications like *The Guardian, Vice* and *Broadly*.

....

To my trans sisters,

As I sat down to write you this letter I watched a news report about a teenage girl in Florida who was swimming. She was attacked by an alligator beneath the water surface. As it sunk its teeth into her leg, she remembered she had been taught once what to do should such a thing ever happen – she put her fingers into the alligator's nostrils so that it couldn't breathe and instead had to release her to draw breath through its mouth. As a result, she survived with only a leg wound which healed. You may wonder why I'm recounting this here, but it's because she has been on a global media tour in which she is being widely praised for her cool, rational thinking when in danger – she did what she had to do to survive against quite overwhelming odds (most people do not survive alligator attacks, the report said).

It's funny because while we haven't wrestled with fearsome creatures beneath the water surface, we perhaps share something with the alligator girl. We have chosen to survive and take steps to survive instead of being pulled under. But we are rarely praised for our survival instinct – it's not seen as such, and our efforts get questioned and devalued. Our choices to live more authentically are seen as confusing, alarming, damaged behaviour by many around us. It is not – we have chosen to survive and we have shown remarkable ingenuity in ensuring that survival. So let me congratulate you on getting here. You have chosen the calmest, sanest and most rational path: living. You won't get congratulated on it much – so if you take one thing from this, it's that we choose to survive in a culture which has not created sufficient opportunities for us to thrive – for that we are all miraculous.

We exist as at least two things this society often shows contempt for: trans people and women. I have tried to tell myself every day to try and live as joyfully as I can in the face of that contempt. Coming out and starting transition is both an end and a beginning. I expected myself to be instantly happier when I came out but suddenly I was faced with new difficulties:

'I am woman' – but no one sees me as one.

'I am free of the masculinity I never asked for and which wounded me so deeply' – but now I must struggle with femininity, how I will embody it and how people will treat me for it.

Negotiating these things will be different for everyone – depending on the support systems we have and the privileges we do or don't have (rich/poor, our racial background, our education etc.) but the easiest way I can explain what transition is like to you is by an analogy (I'm a wanky writer so apologies for that):

Coming out and starting physical transition is like seeing a ship in the distance that will rescue you – initially it's euphoric like 'omg a boat yes – I'm getting off this', but the boat is actually hours away from you and doesn't always move in a straight line towards the island so you start to fixate on it – obsess more about its movements and get driven crazy every second by how slow and long it's taking and you start to curse at the boat and it also makes you more angry at the island and even the things you liked about it when there was nothing else become really intolerable – it feels worse than before and you can't enjoy any of it because you're just obsessed with the boat's movements and when it's finally going to arrive. Obsessed with how passing you are, obsessed with how pretty you are, obsessed with getting this procedure or that surgery, obsessed obsessed OBSESSED!

So my first piece of advice: try not to obsess. It's easy to throw yourself into 'Being Trans' as if it's a full-time job – but you were a person before transition and that person had interests, passions and desires outside of her gender. Try to think about balance. Seek out friendships – online or IRL – with other trans women, but continue to invest in the cis friends who support you and make you feel good. Read articles and books about transition but read other things too. Learn to look at yourself dead on in the mirror once a day – but don't look every time you pass one. Don't stand for bullshit – but don't go looking for transphobia online or elsewhere. That last one was important – I felt I had to understand and rationalise perfectly why some people (men, trans exclusionary feminists, whoever...) seem to hate us so much. DON'T. We know full well some people hate us, sis – why did I go looking for it? Why did I try and argue my existence with bigots? Why did I trigger my own mental health problems?

That's another thing – it's likely that being trans leaves us all with trauma and mental health problems. I am a recovering alcoholic and self-harmer with a severe depressive disorder and anxiety. Walking down the street as a clockable trans woman for the first year of my transition didn't help with any of this. If anything it made it worse – you need to see mental health problems as a related but separate problem to tackle. Hormones or tits are great – but they won't stop you drinking or using or cutting or starving yourself or bingeing. Try and see transition not as a cure-all but as a starting point from which you can work on making yourself a whole person – you might not be ready to stop now but maybe you will be in a month, what do you think you could do to get you closer to that point? Cis people don't see all of their problems through the lens of their gender; nor should we.

Some final things that I know are really tough (I haven't always followed them) but let's keep it real:

Romantically and sexually? You deserve better than anyone who makes you feel grateful for their attention. You also deserve better than anyone who only treats you as an exciting detour in their own desires. Have sex with them if you want and don't feel bad about wanting to be desired but ALWAYS remember what you deserve.

Don't compare yourself to other trans women on looks – we're women and beauty is a cultural value designed to make women compete with each other and hate each other. Try to resist it!

Hand people's shame back to them. Refuse it – say no, in whatever small way you can. We were raised on shame handed to us – every time you feel ashamed about who you are ask yourself 'how can I hand the shame back?'

Finally, I'll finish as I began: congratulations for choosing the conditions of your own existence and survival when no one ever showed you how. You bossed the hardest dilemma of all: whether to live. Remember Hamlet? 'To be or not to be – that is the question.' There's a reason it's one of the most famous lines ever written, hun. You chose to be. You are going to be fine.

Shon Faye

Roz Kaveney

....

Roz Kaveney is a LAMBDA-winning writer, poet and critic. She graduated from the University of Oxford in 1973, co-founded Feminists Against Censorship in 1989 and was also elected to Executive of Liberty (the National Council for Civil Liberties) in the early 1990s, serving as Deputy Chair until 1999. Roz was part of the Trans Parliamentary Forum in the early 2000s that worked on the Gender Recognition Act and was part of the TransLondon delegation to the Equality and Human Rights Commission working on the Equalities Act 2010; she also helped to organise various demonstrations against transphobia during the 2000s.

....

Three times as old as you have been alive

Your aunt and sister. You don't know my name

Perhaps. Still kin. Important details the same.

I prove that you will probably survive.

Of course things as they are no guarantee

I sometimes wonder quite how I'm still here.

Drink sex and drugs. So many disappear.

Who'd counsel wiser kinder far than me.

But I am what you get. Be good at things

As well as who you'll be. Let love be deep

Not just for lucky ones with whom you'll sleep.

And pay attention when some sweetness sings

Soft in your heart. Our life of moments made

So take this step. Be you. Don't be afraid.

Roz Kaveney

Amazon Eve

....

Amazon Eve is an American model and actress, named the world's tallest model by the Guinness World Records. She was photographed by Karl Lagerfeld for the 2013 September issue of *Harper's Bazaar* alongside Scarlett Johansson and Carmen Dell'Orefice, and has also posed on the cover of popular Australian magazine, *Zoo Weekly*. She had a recurring role on the popular TV series American *Horror Story: Freak Show* and is an advocate for LGBT and children's rights.

....

To my trans sisters,

It's not about whether you pass or not. It's not about whether you look a certain way or not. Don't fetishize the female form onto your own. Accept your own form with realistic expectations; self-acceptance is key whatever the final result. Get used to your image in the mirror, you will not look the way you would have if you transitioned prior to male puberty; sorry, just the way it is. You have to want this more than you want to breath at this stage of life, otherwise don't do it. Also keep in mind that the more surgeries you undergo to achieve some unrealistic Barbie doll look, the more instability you'll have in kinetic chain.

This is the stuff they don't tell you when you're about ten years into transition about gender dysphoria. You may still have debilitating gender dysphoria even after you finish with all the physical changes, depending on when you begin transitioning. Being visibly trans sucks, it has improved over time and it's much better than it was even ten years ago; however, it's a shit sandwich for the rest of your life if you don't assimilate well. It's a form of psycho-social death for your old self. Are you ready for that? You have to be ready for people being mean to you everyday you walk out that door. You may lose friends or family. Be strong. Say to yourself, 'I don't care what people think.'

I can best describe it this way: It's a complete kinetic chain reboot best done prior to puberty, so learn to be grateful for what you have and not be resentful for what you don't. Resentment will kill your spirit. I'm not a transition coach though, read up about this, it's all available online, therapy helps too. Your therapist is who you should be giving all your problems, frustrations and insecurities to. Write in a journal.

Don't take transition lightly. This is a serious issue, If this isn't something that manifested in you from a when you were little, it's probably not legitimate. Don't let a fetish, multiple-borderline personality disorder, mid-life crisis or schizophrenia run amok with your mental health. It's your job to manage this, no one else's. It's why you seek therapy during the beginning of transition – to make sure this doesn't manifest as something else. If it's something you feel certain about and fear is the reason you didn't transition when you were younger, that's understandable. It was 1984 and I was 16, during the AIDS epidemic, Reagan was in office and our healthcare was shut down. I was scared to death. I had good reason. I'm probably alive today because I waited to transition later in life, but I have to always remember I was always transgender from birth.

Our problem is fear. It's not the hate out there, we think it's hate; it's fear. No one can help you but you, you need your own courage right now. No one else can give that to you. I'm not going to be a cheerleader. I suggest you avoid them.

Trans people who grow up in emotionally withholding environments, who experience abuse, sexual assault or physical trauma along their journeys, the damage to a transgender child's sense of self-worth and self-esteem can be tremendous, reaching far into their adulthood. The hard part in recovery is removing the damaging factors, and doing the work that needs to be done to rebuild sense of self-worth, increase self-esteem, and find validation from within so that one doesn't need to seek this validation from others. This work was painful and difficult for me, required tremendous strength and courage, and often involves 'rewiring' decades of patterns of thought and feelings that go to the very core of one's sense of self and my place in the world.

I know what it's like to be in that dark place. The answer is love and self-acceptance.

I recommend a strong network of positive people who supply support and affirming messages as a place to draw inspiration, to remember that you're not alone on this journey, and to reinforce your path out of that place of low self-worth, discovering your amazing self. It's how Amazon Eve was born. Be patient. Be brave. Allow your gratitude and appreciation of your gifts to speak to many other transgender people, and echo what we are all trying to achieve – mental equilibrium and a sense of peace of mind for all of us.

Most of all love yourself.

Amazon Eve

Abi Austen

....

Abi Austen is the first officer in the British Army to complete gender reassignment from male to female. Although others in the Royal Navy and Royal Air Force have successfully transitioned in the service, as the first officer and first paratrooper, Abigail's transition caused a media frenzy. After a lengthy legal battle, she was forced to leave the British Army, but years later joined NATO forces in Kandahar Province, Afghanistan —said to be the most dangerous place on earth. In 2008 Abigail was the subject of a documentary on Channel 4 entitled *Sex Change Soldier* and authored the book *Lord Roberts' Valet* about her time in Afghanistan.

....

To Ian – the man I used to be,

You don't know me, because you have not yet decided to let me live. But you always knew I was there. I am the voice that lived inside your head all your life. The voice that you put into a box and hid on the back shelf of your consciousness.

I am Abi, the person you will become. I am writing to you ten years after I left that form behind on the operating table in Chonburi, Thailand.

I want to thank you for sustaining me for all these years. I had an incredible life because of you that would not have been possible had Abi lived and breathed from the beginning.

But I also want to say 'sorry' to you, for all the pain having me inside you all those years must have caused. Only we know how many relationships failed, how many careers crashed and burned and how many times you came close to ending it all because of my persistent voice.

You were the skin I inherited but never owned.

I honour your memory for those times.

But I want you to know that it all came good. In these past ten years, despite all the growing pains of a new life in middle-age, I am truly happy.

Becoming Abi saved us both. For, although I am now the woman you knew lived within you, I retain Ian's talent and drive for life. Back then, it was used to merely survive. Now, I put it to good use.

I am sorry our family decided to reject Abi. But that is their loss. They do not know what a complete person I have become.

This has been a journey to self-actualisation. You carried me to the point of departure. Now, I finally breathe.

It is all good, Ian. You will never be forgotten, but all that you were is now complete.

I am Abi Austen, woman.

Deal with that, World.

Abi Austen

Helen Belcher

....

Helen Belcher is a British trans rights campaigner. As a member of the UK Parliamentary Forum on Gender Identity, she presented a substantial amount of evidence to the Leveson Inquiry about transphobia in the media and also to the Parliamentary Inquiry in 2015. She is one of the founders of Trans Media Watch, a charity that aims to improve media coverage of trans and intersex issues. Helen was recognised by the *Independent on Sunday* as one of the most influential LGBT people in the UK for three years running.

....

Dear me,

So you're 14, just found Jesus, and that's giving you some solace in this Victorian boarding school. Your new-found faith has empowered you to stop being a victim and you're making a real effort to smarten up and do the right thing. And that's all great.

Forty years on – I know what lies ahead for you: the sunny uplands and the dim lowlands; learning what love is and what it isn't; the growing to understand yourself and understanding that you have to grow.

If I challenge your faith, you're going to reject me. Your loyalty is born out of your stubbornness – and that doesn't change. But it will hold you in good stead.

So I will say, in terms that you will understand, that your God knows you and loves you – all of you. Your God doesn't make mistakes, and that 'itch', your 'thorn of the flesh', is part of you – so, in your terms, it's made by God. It doesn't go away. Forty years on, we call it 'trans'.

Yes, I know you'll be interpreting the 'to him who overcomes' verse as overcoming this weakness – but it's not a weakness, and what you have to overcome is not this.

Right now you feel alone – you think no one understands, and you can't open up to anyone. You're still learning to act the part. I understand. The late '70s is not a great time to be different, and a single-sex boarding school is not a great place to be different either. Things will get better, but not for a while.

But you are not alone. There are others, many others, who are struggling like you are. The boys around you – they also have their own problems. No one is perfect, not even the popular ones, or the ones who used to beat you up. They all feel inadequate in their own ways, and are trying to find who they are as well.

What I would say is: 'Don't be afraid of commitment.' You can make decisions, and you can change them. There's very little that can't be undone. You will never be able to see all the consequences. Whenever you try to map something out, don't try to predict the outcome, but rather think about what happens if various things happen as a result. Your terror makes you want to control. You'll find out that you can't control, and you don't need to be terrified.

When you go to university, do try to broaden your horizons. There's a whole bunch of stuff that will go on which will help, if you let it. When you get older, you realise that you regret the things you didn't do. Do them. Go caving. Find the New Romantics. Join the choral society. When politics becomes interesting, as it will do in a few years, think about getting involved, even if you decide that you need to leave later on.

You will see that you're drawn to things that you can become good at: teaching, speaking, acting, campaigning. That interest in science and space – don't be afraid to take off the blinkers imposed by your faith (I won't say religion). You're discovering computers. They'll help you earn money and you'll learn to be pretty good with them. Others won't understand and will try to channel you in different ways to them, but you don't think the same way as them.

I know your daydreams – I dreamt them. You will stop dreaming them, because you'll become frightened by them. But the two main ones, being female and standing for Parliament – yeah, they can happen. Yes, it's terrifying at times, but it's exciting – it's living.

And, even though you question this, you are not unlovely or unloved. You will have a wife, and two fantastic children. They believe in you – even if they think you're a bit mad. And your current family, they know more than you think they do. You can still shock them, but they know you, especially Mum.

I can't say there won't be pain, but you will find a way through. You will learn to believe in yourself. That stubbornness, which is making you doubt this letter, can be channelled to make things better for others too.

Above all, you can make a difference – to society, to your family, to you. Don't be afraid to be that change. Don't be afraid to live. Choose life.

With much love,
Helen

Kate Hutchinson

....

Kate Hutchinson is the CEO of the trans and gender-variant education and awareness organisation Wipe Out Transphobia, which operates one of the largest social network pages in the world focused on the subject. She is also a trustee of the Welsh LGBT charity Unity Group Wales, a facilitator for All About Trans and a founding member of the Trans Equality Legal Initiative and delivers training on their behalf. She also provides training across the UK to an array of charities and institutions including the National Health Service (NHS). Kate has recently been nominated for the positive role model award at the National Diversity Awards. Aside from her work for the LGBT+ community she is a passionate rock musician.

....

To my trans sisters,

I bet right now you have a million things going through your mind – fears, hopes, dreams. So the first thing I want to say – very important this – is breathe! Just sit and breathe.

I know it's probably a scary time for you right now, but also exciting.

My first days of wandering out into the world as my authentic self were mostly spent standing by the back door of my house, trying to summon up the nerve to push down on that door handle and step forward into the light. Most of the time I would quickly run back into the bathroom to check my hair and make-up again, hoping I looked 'passable'. There were usually numerous trips to the door and back to the mirror before I stepped out, but I got there in the end.

My heart was in my mouth a lot in those early days of transition. Worried about being accepted, about passing. Then I went with the bright red hair.

I wear a wig, it's no secret. My natural hair is long and blond, but unfortunately I have a receding hairline that testosterone gave me. I tried various styles, colours, lengths. Then I saw the long red wig on Ebay (of all places). When I tried it on my head it was immediately obvious, this was me.

Yes it was beautiful, but it threw up another insecurity for me. The fact is that it was bright red and would draw attention to me when I was trying to blend in, trying to pass.

I was getting sick to death by this point of the pressure to 'pass' and blend into society. I have never followed the crowd to be honest. I have always been a rebel, a gob on legs and too stubborn for my own good at times. I am a musician and have played in rock bands since I was old enough to hold an electric bass. Rebellion comes with the territory.

So I thought, I love this hair and I'll be fucked if I'm going to let some judgemental folks' attitudes prevent me from looking the way I want to.

Eventually I got up the nerve to go out with the red hair, I went charity shop trawling in a local town, super self-conscious of the bright red beacon on my head. Then I started to realise no one cared... That was, until I got to the local market. As I walked through I looked ahead and I could see one of the stall holders with his stare fixed on me like a camera tracking from about 30 metres away. I realised I was going to be walking right past him. My heart rate increased, my mouth was dry, my anxiety starting to get a grip. That was the point when Katie Lou Chaos really found herself. Something in my head said, 'NO! You do not have to take this shit. You are not going to let somebody else's issue ruin your day.'

This was the moment when I decided the concept of 'passing' would never stop me from expressing myself in a way that felt good and authentic to me. I would always be my truthful self and not what someone expected me to be.

I looked at the guy ahead. I took a deep breath, fixed my gaze on him and carried on walking. When I got alongside him and he was still staring, I stopped dead. I looked him directly in the eyes and smiled the biggest smile I could.

I have never seen somebody look so embarrassed. He turned his gaze away immediately. I didn't shout or scream, I just smiled and it took his power away. I felt empowered. My confidence soared.

That was the moment that set me free, the moment when I didn't have to apologise for who I was anymore. That was the beginning of my true authenticity.

So if you're standing there, at the beginning of your transition, looking in the mirror wondering how the hell you are going to get through this, just take a look at yourself, take a breath and smile – this does get easier. It might be easy to say for me a few years down the line, but don't get too worried about the whole passing thing. You'll realise soon enough it doesn't mean a thing. What is important is that you are happy and comfortable with yourself, that others' attitudes towards you are their problems, not yours. Keep being your awesome self and you won't go far wrong. Your confidence will build and you will be unstoppable.

Rock your authentic self.

Kate Hutchinson

Juno Roche

....

Juno Roche is a campaigner, writer and former teacher who came to prominence after giving a speech about the discrimination transgender teachers face, at the National Union of Teachers annual conference. She received a standing ovation and trended on Twitter. She was given the Blair Peach Award for outstanding contribution to equalities and appeared on the *Independent on Sunday*'s annual Rainbow List and World Pride Power List. She now writes about trans issues regularly for *Refinery29* and the *Huffington Post* and is working on her first book. Juno was recently shortlisted for Campaigner of the Year at the European Diversity Awards.

....

To my trans sisters,

You were born radical, you were born beautiful, you were born woman enough. Please don't spend your whole life trying to live up to impossible standards of femininity. You have things to do, places to go and people to meet. Remember to enjoy your bravery, bask in your authenticity and truly feel the sun on your face.

Your very being makes this a better world.

Love,

Juno

Alexandra Grey

....

Alexandra Grey is an American actress, best known for her role as Elizah Edwards on the Golden Globe-winning hit TV series *Transparent*. She has also starred in the CBS legal drama *Doubt*, alongside Laverne Cox, and on Comedy Central's *Drunk History*, portraying Marsha P. Johnson (her episode has been nominated for a GLAAD Media Award). It was recently announced that she has been cast in ABC's *When We Rise*, directed by Oscar winner Dustin Lance Black (2017).

....

To my trans sisters,

Transitioning is such a touchy topic. I'm thinking of the most genuine advice I can give. I'd say, 'Understand that this is a life-changing decision – understand that your life will forever be changed!' I could tell you that you're going to be so happy and life is going to be beautiful and filled with so much joy, but I'd rather be real with you. When you transition, internally you're going to be so happy in this new authentic body, but know that we as trans people are in crisis. We are still fighting for our basic human rights. So I want you to be prepared to live this new life but to just know that we have so much work to do before society begins to truly understand that we are here and we're here to stay. I'd say to you to take your time transitioning. Know that less is always more and you have the rest of your life to live and be who you always were. Find your purpose! I struggled with this starting out, because you're taught to believe transition is all about hair and make-up, pass-ability, and a bunch of other crazy things. I grew out of that quickly! Your purpose shouldn't be to wear the highest heels or to have the biggest muscles. Your purpose should be to open hearts and minds, to make this world a better place for someone else as long as you are here. Most of all be free, live like there's no tomorrow and be love.

XOXO

Alexandra G

Erin Swenson

....

Erin Swenson is the first-known mainstream Protestant minister to transition and retain ordained office, making national headlines when she did so in 1996. Erin currently serves on the Religion Council for the Human Rights Campaign in Washington, DC, and speaks both nationally and internationally on trans and religious issues. Erin earned the Outstanding Service to the State Award for her work with the Georgia State Legislature, and the Presbyterian Synod of Southern California and Hawaii presented her with the prestigious Lazarus Award in 2005 for her outstanding advocacy for transgender people across the country. Since turning 60, she has completed 36 triathlons.

....

To my trans sisters,

So you are making a gender transition in the second decade of the 21st century! First, I offer my congratulations because it takes courage, foresight and faith to do this. The world is still not a friendly place for us, so making the decision to live authentically is perhaps one of the most significant things you will ever do. It was for me. I offer you three gifts in celebration of your transition:

a picture of your family, a lesson for survival and, finally, a good word (in olden times they called it a *benediction*).

First, the picture. It's one of those intergenerational family portraits and there are many faces. Like most family portraits, it comes with a story. I was a ten-year-old boy living in suburban Atlanta, Georgia, when I first had the thought that I wanted to be a girl. At the time I had heard no one say anything about this kind of desire, and it made me feel very lonely. I decided to keep it as a secret because I had no idea what would happen if I told my parents. It was one day as I was cleaning up the newspapers (one of my household chores) that I saw a story about a US Marine who had become a bride after a 'sex change'. They called it *transsexualism*. I was transfixed. Though I still couldn't say anything to anybody, this gave me relief because I knew that I was not uniquely broken. So, our family portrait includes her picture, with a white wedding dress and flowers.

This experience opened up a world for me. I quickly learned how to use the *Reader's Guide to Periodical Literature* (a book we used to use way before the Internet and Google), and a world of transsexuals opened up for me. Soon I was learning about how people have been walking this path for a very long time. I learned of Christine Jorgensen, who made a very public gender transition (back then it really was called a 'sex change') and started all kinds of dialogue. Then there was Jan Morris, the writer who had, as a man, been on Hillary's expedition to climb Mount Everest. No one had ever successfully done it at the time, and knowing that someone like me had done such a courageous thing was a real boost. I learned about a doctor, Richard Raskind, who struggled mightily with himself and his family before coming to accept herself, becoming Renée Richards. All these people, and many more, are part of the family portrait. There was Sylvia Rivera, who has been called the Rosa Parks of the transgender movement, and Jamison Green who inspired scores of transmen. So many others, and the picture isn't complete without all of the thousands of people who courageously and openly broke gender norms, and in so doing shaped a world that has eventually led to the acceptance you enjoy today.

It's a large portrait, indeed, and your picture is among the multitudes as you are now part of our family. So much to be proud of!

Second comes the survival lesson. Gender transition is one of the most complex and challenging things that a person can accomplish. It's very easy to get caught up in the multitude of things that need to be done, and to be discouraged when it doesn't go as well as planned. My belly ached with anxiety; would I be successful? I obsessed over small physical characteristics that seemed like mountains in my way. I would never be able to live as a woman! People who wavered in their support of me inhabited my nightmares. And then there was the Church.

Most transgender and gender non-conforming people come from some kind of religious background. For many it seems an optional journey not worth the trouble because faith groups often do not understand and don't want to. For me it was different. For me the idea that God loves me, even with all my secrecy, strangeness and despair, was essential from the earliest memories of my gender struggle. As a result, I was ordained (as a man) as a minister by the Presbyterian Church in 1973 and worked as a counselor under that ordination my whole adult life. And I needed to retain that ordination through my transition because my family's health insurance was directly linked to my ordination. Losing my ordination would literally place my daughters' lives at risk. The stakes were high, and I would have to get the Church to accept my gender change at any cost.

Then one day I was gazing in the mirror, looking at my growing hair and smooth face, and for early signs of the effects of hormonal treatment. I caught the look of fear in my eyes. It all seemed so impossible. I couldn't become a woman and have the Church agree with my change. Still in front of the mirror I began to cry, believing that I would soon give up. Then I looked at my own eyes more deeply. I remembered that Shakespeare wrote that the eyes are the window to your soul. I looked more deeply, and then I realized it. I realized that my eyes have always been the eyes of a woman, that I have seen the world all my life through my woman's eyes. And I realized further that it would always be that way for me; no matter what gender I presented with the rest of my body, I would always be a woman. It was a powerful moment of self-acceptance. All the worry about facial hair, broad shoulders and my general masculine shape dissolved into my new realization that I am a woman, no matter what.

And it was when I accepted myself that I could relax and stop trying to be something I was not. I became convinced of my womanhood against all odds and I would live into that reality. I could play with clothes and make-up, but they were not essential. I could take hormones, but the success or failure of my feminization made no difference. I am a woman.

And you know, the Church pretty much had to go along with it. Accepting and being your authentic self is powerful.

Finally, a good word for you. Persevere. It means to remain faithful to yourself, no matter what. It requires no specific course of action except that you insist on being who you really are. It's an inoculation against suicidal despair that can get you through the darkest of nights. And please, do, take good care of yourself and thrive. It is, in the end, the only way you can be a loving human being.

With love,

Erin Swenson

Kristine W. Holt

....

Kristine W. Holt is an American lawyer, activist, speaker and author. A graduate of Temple University School of Law, she has dedicated a great deal of her career to serving the LGBT community, defending us and our rights in court. She has been the recipient of several academic awards, including the CALI Excellence for the Future Award for Legal Writing and Research. In 1995 Kristine ran in the Democratic primary for her local county office, and was placed fourth out of seven candidates. In 1997 she published *Re-evaluating Holloway: Title VII, Equal Protection, and the Evolution of a Transgender Jurisprudence*.

....

To my trans sisters,

You stand in a position where I was many years ago, stepping off on a journey few people travel. Rest assured, while your companions may be few, you will not travel alone. And while you may travel with others, your future will be solely what YOU make of it.

It is a good thing to meet others like yourself, younger and older, and drink in all their experiences. Everyone has something to share with you, and you, in turn, will share with them what you have discovered. Soon, you'll find someone you come to respect and seek them out for their special wisdom. Take what you can use. You may later find that your 'mentor' has clay feet; it happened to me. That's okay, though, and it is just part of learning what authenticity is all about. Embrace it where you can find it. (As Polonius advised his child, Laertes, who was just setting forth upon his own journey: 'To thine own self be true, and it must follow, as the night the day, thou canst not then be false to any man.') Many other fellow travelers will come into and out of your life, eager to share something with you, for good or for bad, even if they don't know it themselves. Graciously accept what they give, and use it as you may.

The journey will be arduous. We are of a kind little understood by the mainstream of humanity. There will be times when you might wish you'd never been born. You may feel at times that you might have made a mistake. Maybe you feel you lack the courage, stamina, resources, support or whatever you need to sustain yourself. I've been there, too. But two thoughts that helped drive me forward were these: there is only one thing in this world that will kill me – everything else I will survive; and where there is life, there is hope. You are a unique creation of the universe, and as such, you have a right to exist. Do the hard legwork, and the universe will deliver for you.

The decision to transition brings with it great opportunities if you can recognize them for what they are. Let me tell you a little about myself: I was fired from my job as an intake worker at a government office after coming out as transgender (or transsexual, as we called it back then). What my employer really gave me was worth much more than what was taken from me. They gave me lots of time to continue my recovery and sobriety, which preceded my decision to transition; time to get involved politically in local government; and time to pursue my legal actions against them, mostly *pro se*, which in turn gave me a new-found appreciation for the law. I contemplated taking on challenges I'd never considered before – such as a primary run for political office. I gained some small bit of regional notoriety, which got picked up by the newswires. Jay Leno provided some humorous commentary on my candidacy a few nights running. Supporters from across the state sent mail to me care of the Office of the Mayor (who was also a kindred Democratic Committee woman). All this was while I was either sleeping in my car or 'house-sitting' for friends. I didn't win (I was placed fourth out of seven), but that wasn't the point. I made a difference in redefining some of the issues in the election – and I gained respect. Respect is good.

After the election, I matriculated to Temple Law School in Philadelphia to pursue my new passion for public service. I received a front page send-off from the local newspaper, with a full-color picture and an upbeat article. It was good to know that, even with the occasional detractors in my hometown of 13,000 people, I had been able to have some influence in public affairs.

At Temple I blossomed! It was a culture shock – my first time living in a large city. The single neighborhood I moved into was more populous than the whole county I'd previously lived in. The city has so many distractions, but I found my purpose and excelled. I was generally known to be transgender among my classmates, but it never seemed to be an impediment to my studies or social life. I was a member of the Women's Law Caucus, and an officer in both the LGBT Civil Rights student group and the Phi Alpha Delta Legal fraternity (a co-ed organization). I was hired as a part-time law clerk by an attorney downtown, and also worked part-time as a judicial clerk for a senior judge in the court system. In my second year, I was selected for the *Temple Law Review*, served as Managing Editor and wrote an article outlining a path to Title VII protection for transgender people. That was in 1997. (You can read the article here: www.holtesq.com/employment. htm.) The Dean himself was one of my advisors. I am happy to say that the reasoning set forth there has been adopted by five US Circuit Courts of Appeal, and also adopted as guidelines by the federal Equal Employment Opportunity Commission. I also won the Smith and Liebel Family Law Graduation Prize for a paper I wrote addressing transgender marriage issues.

Upon graduation *cum laude*, I took a year-long law clerk's position with an appellate judge in the state system. The wages I earned while working for the state court provided me with the final financial resources to book my surgery with Dr. Brassard in Montreal, set for September 13, 1999 – the day before my 43rd birthday. Following that, I returned to the office of the attorney I'd worked part-time for as a student, who then set me up in my own office for nominal rent, with a contract for doing research and brief writing. I hung my shingle and started growing my own book of business. Within the span of seven years I had transformed myself from an often-drunk, withdrawn and surly individual to a socially active, outgoing, and productive scholar and professional, who has made a meaningful contribution to current jurisprudence and public policy – and to the lives of those around me.

Do the hard legwork, and the universe will deliver for you.

I also came to realize the metaphysical truth of this principle on the eve of the final step of my journey. While I was in Montreal for two weeks for sex reassignment surgery (SRS), I maintained regular contact with so many of my family members and friends through daily emails, sharing my thoughts and experiences as I progressed forward. An excerpt from my email written the evening before taking that last step reads:

> Okay. Well. Here I am, in the hospital. I am checked in and had my second enema. All paperwork signed. A cup of chamomile and a sleeping tablet in a small paper cup sits on my bed desk. I take it. I awake around 6 am. I talk with the surgeon and the anesthesiologist. We walk upstairs to the operating theater. I get a shot. I climb onto the table; I fall asleep; I wake up a girl. Very easy. Very painful. Very necessary... I look in my meditations book for tomorrow and it says: "'Nobody told me how hard and lonely change is." Courage to change accompanies faith. My fears are telling me to look within the spiritual source of strength, ever present but often forgotten' (Joan Gilbertson, quoted in Karen Casey, 1982, *Each Day A New Beginning*). How a propos. Also bookmarked at the page is a fortune cookie message carelessly placed there some years in the past; faded and yellowed, it says: 'Smile when you are ready.' I laugh! I am more than ready – I am eager. I have screwed my courage to the sticking place, and it hangs there now unattended. I eat a couple tea biscuits, drink another cup of chamomile. Soon I'll take the pill and fall into the chrysalis of pain, to emerge a day later as...me.

The whole Universe was telling me it was okay to take that necessary step. How can you resist that??? If you are authentic in your course, you too will find your courage and your sticking place.

But a funny thing happened when I came out of that chrysalis the next day – life continued on, for that day and all the days afterward! But now, I had life largely unbedeviled by inner turmoil, self-loathing, and all the other nagging doubts we create for ourselves before we become whole. Through the process of becoming me, I found purpose to my life, and ultimately, the love of, and for, another blessed soul. I have three adult children who weathered my storm, and have graced me with the joys of a half-dozen grandchildren, who love their grandma in turn. It didn't come easy, but nothing worthwhile does. You'll find that the process of 'becoming' is just as important as 'being' – if not more so. It forms the basis of all you will be. Because in the end, you are who you are.

Do it well, and you will be well. Do it with authenticity, and you will be authentic. 'To thine own self be true...' You'll certainly be stronger and happier for it.

And I wish this happiness for you, too.

Sincerely,

Kristine W. Holt

Pari Roehi

....

Pari Roehi came to prominence after starring on Germany's *Next Top Model* in 2015, sharing her story with millions of viewers on German television. Since the show, she has used her platform and popularity to educate the masses on what it means to be transgender, being featured everywhere from *i-D* magazine to *OK!* magazine, and continues to do so using her popular YouTube videos. Pari has just released her biography *Mein bunter Schatten: Lebensweg einer Transgender-Frau* (*My Colourful Shadow: The Life of a Transgender Woman*, 2016).

....

To my trans sisters,

I'm sitting here at my computer, thinking about my journey and the warnings and lessons I wish another experienced trans woman would have shared with me when I began my transition.

Looking back, I have made many mistakes during my transition, I've fallen flat on my face and made many wrong choices, but all of these experiences made me the strong young woman I am today.

I was blessed to have an accepting and supporting family and I was brought up in a very privileged LGBTQ accepting country (the Netherlands). This all gave me the freedom to experiment and to experience life in all its glory.

I truly realise that many of my trans sisters reading this letter don't have these privileges and that life can be very hard and unfair sometimes. Even though I received love and support from family and friends during my transition, I also had to deal with a lot of ignorance and pain from the outside world. I know how it feels to be rejected by society, to be bullied and harassed, to be beaten and disrespected; but all of these experiences taught me to fight back with class, be strong and to not give up.

The greatest lesson I have learned from my wonderful mother is to dream, dream big and speak it in to the universe. Work hard and surround yourself with positive people who uplift you and give you a good feeling about yourself. Know that YOU have the power to make your dreams come true. It's never too late to achieve your goals. You get a long way with hard work and determination.

My wish for you is happiness and self-love. From my experience, happiness can be found by experimenting and giving yourself the freedom to make mistakes in life. Don't be too harsh on yourself. Self-love is something I'm still working very hard on but this is a journey I have embraced with open arms. I take it day by day, and this is the advice I would like to give you. Don't rush, take it easy...

Give yourself the time to live, love and laugh but also to make mistakes. At the end of the day you can't expect love and acceptance from others if you can't love yourself to the fullest.

Stand straight, young lady, keep ya chin up, take a big breath and go out there. Don't forget you're a goddess and you are not alone!

Much love!

Pari Roehi

Babs Siperstein

....

Babs Siperstein is a member of the Executive Committee of the Democratic National Committee, Vice President of the bipartisan Women's Political Caucus of New Jersey and Political Director of the Gender Rights Advocacy Association of New Jersey. She was New Jersey's first transgender delegate to the Democratic National Convention. Over the years she has been honoured with many awards for her work, including The Pride Network's Stonewall Legacy Award and the American Conference on Diversity's Advocacy Humanitarian Award, and was the first recipient of the Garden State Equality's John Adler Icon of Equality Award.

....

To my trans sisters,

Denial can be extremely powerful, but the truth can set you free!

Somehow I always knew that I was different, but growing up as the first-born male of a first-born male there were certain expectations, plus being one of only two Jewish families in a working-class Irish and Italian neighborhood in Jersey City, New Jersey, I learned to survive and thrive by my wits and sometimes by my fists. I was a 'Jersey guy'!

I grew up before television; we listened to the radio and we read. My mother had a medical encyclopedia and for some reason I was fascinated reading about hermaphrodites and the duality of sex and gender. I recall being fascinated reading about Christine Jorgensen. There were times in my pre-adolescence and adolescence I would fanaticize that I was a woman, wishing that I was...but then I would bury that, those thoughts. I was not effeminate, I was attracted to women.

As I approached my mid-forties, I had my own mid-life crisis. Times were pretty good – I was married with three children, business was pretty good, I had the expensive adult boy toys, a new Jaguar, we had race horses, we were able to travel – but there was something missing and I didn't know what it was. It was like an itch that didn't go away.

I'm very fortunate that my wife, Carol, was my best friend and after I realized that the female part of me had to emerge I had the confidence to share it with her, not yet knowing how far it might go, nor how she would react. Carol was the kind of person who would make lemonade out of a lemon, and from the late 1980s we explored my female side and persona and eventual growth as a woman. As we were both people-friendly and gregarious, we sought out other middle-aged, middle-class couples where the husband was to some degree trans, in order to socialize, starting with meeting at gay clubs and restaurants, then weekends at gay resorts and straight resorts and traveling together on cruises and organizing our groups on cruises. We had an informal group of friends, couples from Toronto, Canada, to Raleigh-Durham, North Carolina. We purchased a small condo on the other side of town, which became my oversized closet and getaway so that the children would not see Babs. We lived a double life while working, running a business as a male, appearing as a male to my horse partners and of course as father to my children.

In 1995 we joined the Imperial Court of New York, became active socially and helped the 501C3 in charity fundraising, eventually becoming the only married husband and wife Princesses! By 1999 and 2000 we were part of the royal family and quite active.

In 2000, a small group of experienced transgender activists invited us to join them in organizing for transgender civil rights. New Jersey had no legislation or even court decisions giving transgender people any protections. In 1992 New Jersey's powerful Law Against Discrimination was amended to give gays and lesbians explicit protections in employment, housing and public accommodations. I was beginning to learn. In the Spring of 2001 the Empire State Pride Agenda (ESPA), New York State's premier gay civil rights organization, reached out to the Imperial Court looking for volunteers to dress up and help raise funds at their big black tie fundraiser that had the new US Senator Hillary Clinton as the featured speaker. I was asked and I volunteered.

That summer of 2001, I was appalled to find out that ESPA, an organization that had no problem seeking transgender and gender-variant gays to help them raise funds, was promoting non-discrimination legislation that protected straight-acting gays and lesbians and whose language excluded transgender people. New York was the home of the Stonewall riots, generally acknowledged as the beginning of the gay political revolution whose heroes were trans people, drag queens and kings – for example, Sylvia Rivera, Marsha P. Johnson, Stormé DeLarverie – these heroes were now being ignored by the NY gay elite! I made a point of attending the historic meeting of New York transgender activists led by Sylvia Rivera with Matt Foreman, Executive Director of ESPA, at the

Metropolitan Community Church in midtown Manhattan. I spoke up, but mostly listened and observed and was totally engaged... I will never forget that day!

As the fall of 2001 approached, my wife of 34 years – my love, my best friend – developed a cough that would not quit, and on October 30, the impossible happened: Carol was gone. She had previously undiagnosed ovarian cancer that had spread to her lungs. Words cannot describe how I felt in my grief...devastated, angry, empty, numb...

I am thankful to a few trans and gay friends who proactively encouraged me to move forward and do things, positive things. As I moved forward and became more aware of the trans rights environment locally and around the country, I soon realized that if gays and lesbians were treated as second-class citizens, it would be at a level way below that I, as a single trans person, would now be perceived and treated. I looked around and saw few or no positive things happening. As a child, when I would complain and be unhappy with a particular situation and my mother thought it was appropriate, she would remind me that 'God helps those that help themselves!'

I focused on channeling my anger and grief. I was trying to keep my business together, to be a responsible parent and grandparent, and to move forward to create transgender rights, observing, reading history, finding and nurturing allies and taking both subtle and bold action when appropriate. In the late spring of 2002, we found out that New Jersey legislature was deliberating the passage of a schools anti-bullying bill. The bill as introduced had language to explicitly protect gay and lesbian students, but trans students were not included. The national organization, the Gay, Lesbian and Straight Education Network (GLSEN), which had advocated the gay language, was unwilling to fight to include transgender language, 'Gender identity/expression', in the bill although the leaders of their local chapters were sympathetic to our cause. We had a little bit of luck as the prime sponsor was my state senator and knew me in my male local business persona. I contacted her, and her chief of staff gave her a story as my late wife was a teacher who was concerned about the bullying of transgender and gender-variant children, and she agreed to add the language in Committee! I must mention Doctor Emanuel Fineberg, AKA Mandee, who was eloquent and moving in her testimony in Committee. The bill was amended in Committee and passed. The assembly took the amended Senate bill and both passed unanimously!

The first success of the Gender Rights Advocacy Association of New Jersey (GRAANJ)! Personally, I needed to do things politically outwardly as Babs. That summer I booked a trip to Southern England. This was partly a matter of closure (it was a tour that Carol and I had planned before she got sick), but also to show to myself, by traveling alone as Babs, that I could fit in with strangers and the public as the woman that I was. Fortunately, I pulled off the trip/tour, although it took a little luck and quick thinking, blaming my travel agent for putting the wrong gender salutation on the booking and no one really looking at my passport photo. (On subsequent travels there were questions at airports, but by then I had the confidence and attitude and knowledge to react in a way that there was no problem.)

I realized that if you want to get things done in politics, you need to get on the inside. You need to get a seat at the table; if you don't have a seat, then you are probably, lunch! Everything that I would now do would be as Babs – everything except work and family events. I joined New Jersey Stonewall Democrats and became active in that group as well as in the Coalition of Gay and Lesbian organizations of which GRAANJ was now a part. I was invited to be part of the leadership of the new Domestic Partnership Task Force, which gave me a history and knowledge of all the activist and political players. In the early fall of 2002, I got involved and took a leadership role working with the Human Rights Campaign (HRC) and the national and state players, helping to elect Frank Lautenberg come back to the US Senate.

Woody Allen once said that 80 percent of success in life is just 'showing up'. I kept on showing up and making connections. It's very true. We passed Domestic Partnership in 2003. By 2004 it was time to work to amend New Jersey's powerful Law Against Discrimination to include 'gender identity or expression' and thus protect trans people from discrimination in employment, housing and public accommodations. The bill was finally introduced in the Assembly in January 2005, but we could not find a sponsor in the Senate. Not even our old friend and local senator would talk to me, not even a senator who was a liberal icon, a freedom rider in the civil rights movement and whose wife and I had mutual social friends. Indeed, even the American Civil Liberties Union (ACLU) would not support it! Why? Because they all assumed that we would fail and in failing we would lose some of the very limited rights that transsexuals had in an appellate court decision. Dr. Enriquez was a physician who ran a medical clinic in South Jersey and was fired when she began to transition on the job as a female. The Court held that, being a transsexual, her firing was covered as 'sex' discrimination. The decision also stated that being a transsexual was a handicap, so she was covered by the disability provision in the statute. A handicap indeed! A handicap only because of the societal stigma, and these liberal gatekeepers refusing to support the bill was clear proof! As a business owner, I needed to see the specific language in black and white on the mandatory posters and they would only be there if we changed the statute.

It was time to switch tactics as some of my influential gay allies were unable to move these and other Senators. I concentrated on getting support from more moderate lawmakers in the Assembly and when we got a former FBI agent, considered to be a conservative Democrat, and our first Republican, a retired Navy Captain who owned several large retail shops, things started to happen. I had helped a friend, a lesbian Democratic operative, with one of her campaigns during the previous fall. She was now working for a freshman state senator and I talked her into sponsoring the bill. She brought a senior senator as a co-prime and we were now on our way! The liberal icons who had earlier refused now had to sign on and they did! The ACLU joined in as well. There were still a great deal of challenges and political dealings and surprises, and I felt as if I earned another Master's degree, but in the end, by December 2006, the bill passed in the shortest period of time of any similar state law and passed by the widest margin 102–8. In the end, I felt that the legislative leaders and the Governor had given us 'respect'!

The next year we quickly and without drama added trans language to the Bias Crimes law, and the year after worked directly with the Department of Motor Vehicles to reform and streamline the policy to change the gender marker on drivers' licenses.

On a national level, I was disappointed that in 2002 neither the prime sponsor of the Employment Non Discrimination Act (ENDA), Barney Frank, nor the largest gay rights advocacy group, HRC, endorsed legislation that was inclusive of transgender people. Although in 2004 I was one of a handful of transgender delegates to the Democratic Nation Convention, Senator Kerry, the party nominee, had no interest in allowing transgender non-discrimination language to be added to the gay language in the party platform. In early 2005, I had the opportunity to engage the Democratic Party and was later invited to join the board of National Stonewall Democrats and eventually chair their Democratic National Committee (DNC) Relations Committee. By 2007, transgender-inclusive language was included in the delegate selection rules for the 2008 convention, and in 2008 the platform contained transgender-inclusive language. In August of 2009, literally minutes before I was confirmed as the first out transgender member of the DNC, the membership amended their Charter and By Laws to include not only transgender non-discrimination language, but also language supporting full inclusion in Democratic Party affairs.

In the Obama administration, transpeople made incredible progress. I acted, when necessary or able, as a bridge to bring administration people together with our outstanding policy wonks, or sometimes as a catalyst to get things moving or just moving faster. In 2012 the White House held its first official Transgender Day of Remembrance, which later morphed to include a forward-looking Transgender Awareness event. When Defense Secretary Ash Carter announced that transgender service members would be able to serve openly, it was the culmination of years when I was part of less than a handful of transgender people directly advocating such changes.

And now Trump and Pence!

Babs Siperstein

Rachael Padman

....

Rachael Padman is Director of Education in the Department of Physics at the University of Cambridge. She studied for her PhD in mm-wave astronomy and instrumentation there in 1977, and has made contributions to research in stellar evolution. In 1996 she was elected as a Fellow of Newnham College, one of the University of Cambridge's all-female colleges, which drew opposition from the likes of Germaine Greer. However, Rachael was rightly supported by the University and kept her fellowship, while Greer resigned from the college administration. In 1998 Rachael was appointed as a lecturer at the University and is currently a member of the University Council and General Board.

....

To my trans sisters,

Charlie has asked us to write a letter to our younger selves. In my case it's a lot younger – I was 27 when I transitioned, 36 years ago, and the world seems quite different now. Every day there is an article in the papers about trans issues; it seems almost as common to hear of trans men as women; the law is on our side. Since 1981 there have been three great pieces of legislation, in the form of the Gender Recognition Act 2004, the Equality Act 2010 and marriage equality in 2014. As a result, we can all be who we want to be, marry whom we want to marry, and are protected from discrimination. So what's the problem?

Well, of course, it's still a big step, or so it seems to me. Everyone else thinks they know who we are, based primarily on the way we present ourselves, which in turn mostly depends on our genitals. Most of us tend to act the part assigned to us, and it does surprise others when we eventually out ourselves to them. The longer you act the part, the less time there is to unlearn it and learn a new one. In retrospect, I wish I had had the courage to tell my parents when I was still at school. I still don't know how they would have responded, but I like to think we would have muddled through. I have a younger friend who just turned up at university the first day as a woman, round about the same time I transitioned, and she has never looked back. I don't regret much, but I do wish I had done that too.

Of course, if I had, I would not now be the same me that is writing. I wonder whether I would still have studied engineering, or whether I might have gone with my first love of physics, or perhaps one of the other loves I didn't recognise then, such as English, classics or mediaeval languages. And if I had chosen differently, the chances I would have come to Cambridge from Australia, and would now be living in a country cottage in Suffolk, would be vanishingly small. We all have many futures.

That leads to a second point. I think I expected the process of transition to be a bit like that of Kipling's Old Man Kangaroo, who asked Big God Nqong to make him 'different from all other animals [...] by five this afternoon'. In fact, I was exactly the same person the day after transition as the day before, and again the day after surgery as the day before. I know that almost everyone perceived that person as male. That sounds depressing, but what I have understood for some time is that transitioning merely created the opportunity to reset the path I was on, and to take a new direction. It created a new default path; it reset other people's expectations as well as my own; it allowed me to become the person I am now, which I could not have done otherwise. You will need patience. It takes a lifetime.

I am privileged to work in Cambridge, where we have incredibly bright and accomplished students from all over the world. A surprising fraction of them are trans – far more than I believed possible given the statistics as I understood them. Part of it is that there are many more ways of *expressing* gender diversity, and I have to say that Cambridge is a very accepting place. So the barriers to coming out as transgendered in some way are low. But the key is that in a place like Cambridge, what everyone values is your brain. And that leads me to my next piece of advice, which is that trans is simply one aspect of your history and personality: it's not, nor should not be, a career. There are a few people – Paris Lees comes to mind – who can occupy themselves productively working for the community they are now part of, but there isn't room there for all of us. And it doesn't pay very well, either.

This is really important. I feel pretty comfortable with where I am now, but, as I say, it's been a long time. For me, and I recognise this might not apply to you, my need then was not to be trans, but as far as possible to be a woman. But I freely confess I didn't know what I meant by that. In the years before I transitioned, I spent hour upon hour discussing my motivations with a few patient friends, but I don't recall bottoming out that issue. Of course, now in my early sixties, I never did get pregnant, or feel at risk of cervical cancer, or get to be anyone's mother, or have any of the other major life events that distinguish women from men. But I have found a spiritual home in a women's college, Newnham, and conclude that 'being a woman' is primarily social. Men and women interact in different ways, and necessarily have many different concerns: I feel comfortable when I am with women in a social situation, and not when the company is too male-dominated. I would guess that is just a reflection of the same behaviours we also observe in the great apes – a deep-seated biological substrate.

It took me forever to get to the point where being trans was not uppermost in my mind every time I talked to someone. Part of that of course is that no amount of surgery was going to make me shorter, or reduce my bone mass, raise my voice or make my hands smaller. But over the years I have met other women who are taller, bigger, or deeper-voiced, or have larger hands, and that helps to reduce the self-consciousness. I do sense a nice positive feedback situation, in which the less I worry, the less I worry others, so the less reason there *is* to worry. There are still odd occasions on which someone will say 'sir', but they usually then say 'oh sorry', and that happens to lots of women... So one definition of 'being a woman' is just being someone that others perceive and interact with as a woman. Of course, people don't hold up a 'femaleness score' card when you do interact with them, so there isn't much direct feedback, and you can go mad looking for it. Security is not having to worry about that.

I only have one more piece of advice. I know it may not be completely welcome, but it's prompted by Jenni Murray's recent admonition that trans women are not 'real' women. Please show some awareness of other people's concerns and cut them some slack, however much it hurts. As I have said elsewhere, all animals are remarkably good at recognising each other's sex. It doesn't take schooling, and we aren't easily fooled. If people subconsciously perceive a contradiction between our bodies and our presentation that is not their fault, and they are not being rude. We can help them resolve that contradiction through our response to their confusion, but it probably doesn't help simply to insist that according to the Gender Recognition Act we are female.

In fact Murray's remarks were quite nuanced: she was concerned by particular transwomen who had transitioned openly and recently, and on the one hand, expected everyone to accept them as if they had never lived as men, and on the other, were pretty unaware of the experiences of most other women from birth, in a world that is still not equal or fair. Whoever you are inside, to others you are, at least initially, a man in a dress. It really can look like the patriarchy is at it again if we just swan into women's space, after a lifetime of male privilege, and then make ourselves at home there. It's probably best not to set oneself up as a feminist guru, or a rape crisis counsellor, or whatever until you have accumulated real experience living life at least in the shadow of discrimination. Was I a 'real woman' when I transitioned? As far as that is a meaningful question, I think not. Am I now? Well, probably still not, but a lot closer. Now that I have lived rather more than half my life as a woman, the male experience I brought with me becomes ever less important. I never did get to where I originally wanted to be, but in retrospect I am happy with where I am.

There are a million other things I could say to you, but a lifetime of teaching has persuaded me that it's only ever possible to get across a very few key points. When I transitioned, there was no real process as such, no Internet, and not much literature (other than Jan Morris' *Conundrum*), so I had to make it up as I went along. On the whole, I am pleased about that. I never wanted too much advice about how to live the rest of my life, and I still prefer to make it up for myself, to make my own decisions and to take responsibility for them. I hope you can take my suggestions here in the spirit in which they're offered – as the accumulated experience of one particular transwoman following one particular path, which may or may not be relevant to you.

Wishing you all the best,

Rachael

Amelia Gapin

....

Amelia Gapin is a runner who has completed more than ten marathons. In 2016 she became the first trans woman to be featured on the cover of popular fitness magazine *Women's Running*, an event that made headlines worldwide from the *Daily Mail* to *People* magazine. She used the platform to shed light on the current state of affairs not only for trans athletes but for trans people in general. Amelia is also former co-founder and CTO of MyTransHealth, a service that helps transgender people access healthcare.

....

To my trans sisters,

I thought my transition was about surviving in my body, but my reality was so much more than that. It was about truly being me and living my life out loud.

We all have our own stories and experiences, but whatever yours is, don't *just* survive. Thrive!

Exist in this world without apology. Pursue the life you want and the life that is yours. Pursue your best self.

Love,
Amelia Gapin

Bex Stinson

....

Bex Stinson is head of trans inclusion at Stonewall, the largest LGBT rights organisation in Europe. Prior to joining Stonewall, Bex worked as a legal barrister, with her primary interest being in gender recognition and how it affects sex-by-deception cases. Bex recently led Stonewall's 'Vision for Change' project to thread trans inclusion throughout the charity, which prior to 2015 only campaigned for LGB people. Bex has a first class Masters in Law and regularly discusses trans issues in the media for publications like the *Independent*, *The Telegraph* and the *Huffington Post*.

....

To my trans sisters,

You're about to go through hell.

It's going to hurt. It will be scary. It's going to feel isolating. You're going to question your sanity, and your very identity.

You will be misgendered by people, some of whom will be the ones you love, if they decide to stick by you. Most will do it out of habit, or as a mistake, but some will purposefully deny your pronouns and your name. Both will hurt you, regardless of how strong you believe yourself to be. Be prepared to feel a wrenching pain deep within.

There will be times when you feel too scared to leave your front door. You will have terrifying moments walking alone in the dark, or using the toilets in the bar. Sometimes you will feel intimidated by those who hurl abuse at you, spit at you in the street, and those who follow you and try to attack you. You'll need to start thinking twice about where you go, and about the company you keep.

People will stare at you and single you out. You will be spotted and given the silent treatment. The staff in shops will snigger at you and pick on your appearance or your voice. Parents will tell their children it's rude to stare at you, and there will be times nobody will sit next to you on the tube. Be ready to face the glares, and to walk it alone.

Someone will say you have a mental illness. People will tell you that you're not right in the head and that you need to get help. Psychiatrists will ask you what toys you used to play with, and how you masturbate. Some will call you a freak, and a few will say that you're sick. Be prepared to face the horrors of intrusive questioning, and to believe you've gone crazy.

Too many people will tell you you're not a woman. You will be called a man in a dress, and be compared to a cocker spaniel. Often you will be told that surgery and make-up cannot make you female and that you're not entitled to appropriate the word 'woman'. Start accepting that you will question your own gender and that you will, at times, believe you're an imposter.

Don't allow your pain to dig too deep. Being misgendered hurts. When it does, it will instantly banish your confidence. Be ready to deal with that feeling, rather than trying to avoid being misgendered. Don't let the fear scare you away. Being afraid for your safety means that you need to learn how to keep yourself safe, rather than shutting yourself away. Let go of all the relationships you're going to lose. Trying to stay connected with those who disapprove of your gender identity will only hold you back. Figure out how to be comfortable on your own. Don't allow others to twist your mind. It's important to come to terms with your thoughts, your emotions, and it's vital that you're self-aware. Cast off any thoughts telling you that your identity is not valid, or that you're incapable of being yourself.

You are going to go through hell. But, that is no reason to be something you are not. Embrace yourself and own your identity. Understand that life will make things very difficult for you and, instead of letting it break you, strengthen your resolve and build up your support network. Chocolate, I might add, is glorious succour.

Don't get hung up on 'passing' or on trying to fit in. Don't think that anyone else's perception of you can damage your worth or invalidate your identity. Be strong. Be resilient. Fight all those fights and love every minute of being yourself. The world, despite everything, is so beautiful, so vivid and so colourful when you can be the real you.

It's worth it. I promise. Being yourself is worth it.

Yours sincerely,

Bex Stinson

Ashley Breathe

....

Ashley Breathe is a singer-songwriter and trans advocate from New York. She is also a founding member of the hit online talk show *T-Time with the Gurlz*. The show discusses topics relating to the trans experience, often focusing on issues affecting trans women of colour, and ran for four seasons with special guests including social media sensation Ts Madison, artist and DJ Juliana Huxtable and ballroom legend Leiomy Maldonado. Ashley, along with her co-hosts, Foxxjazell and Gia Manmade (and formerly Milan Zanotti), used their platform and popularity with the show to put on events aiding the trans community in the New York area.

....

To my trans sisters,

My name is Ashley Breathe. I chose the last name 'Breathe' because transitioning was a rebirth to me – I felt I was living and breathing as the real me, as my authentic self.

Growing up, I faked masculinity for years. I never could fit in with the boys; I was called 'faggot' at an early age before I even knew what it meant. I was the only child of a single teenage mother – all I knew was my mother. I looked up to her and knew

I wanted to be beautiful like her. I had girlfriends throughout my school years. I pretended I liked them but really I just wanted to study them and be like them, I admired all things girly, and being friends with girls was the closest thing I felt I could achieve.

Once I began working in a retail job at a women's clothing store, I would sneak women's clothes home, and one day my mom found all my girl clothes and threw them in the trash. She and her homophobic husband raided my room of all my female clothes and wigs, which I was hiding under my bed. I felt my womanhood stripped from me, I was told: 'If you want to be a bitch, be it in the streets.' My mother's husband would always call me 'sissy', 'homo', 'bitch', and my mother allowed it. He came into the picture when I was nine, so I was being called a faggot in school and at home... going through all the verbal abuse and trauma.

I began to find a escape in writing. I loved music and I used to stare into the mirror and pretend I was Madonna singing 'Express Yourself', wishing one day I could do the same thing. Being pushed out of home at 17 for my gender identity was tough and that's when I was introduced to sex work. I was looking for acceptance, and I wanted to feel love. I did what I had to do to survive. If my mother had been a bit more tolerant and knowledgeable of transgenderism, she probably wouldn't have kicked me out, but it was just 'I don't understand, so let's get rid of the problem.'

Years later, I managed to find stability on my own. I saved up my sex work money for the better – I have everything of my own. I now advocate for trans empowerment, throwing events for homeless trans youth and doing sit-downs with people going through disownment. With being more stable I have been able to become a successful songwriter working with LGBT artists in the community.

Stay brave! It's always good to have someone to talk to, to help you get through things, because not all transitions are smooth; but I'm glad I went through what I did, because I learnt at a young age that the world is a tough place, you have to be unbreakable to survive, and you can create your own family.

So be safe, stay grounded, and much love, sis.

Ashley Breathe xx

Jessica Mink

....

Jessica Mink is an astronomer and software developer at the Smithsonian Astrophysical Observatory, perhaps best known for co-discovering the rings of Uranus. Her work on occultation predictions also led to the discovery of Neptune's rings and the detection of the extent of Pluto's atmosphere. She also worked on the Space Shuttle Spacelab 2 Infrared Telescope, developing some key workstation and mapping software and pipelines for ground-based spectrographs. Jessica also wrote the commonly used software packages WCSTools and RVSAO.

....

To my trans sisters,

The main things that I can say about transition are that it's an adventure, so you can't predict what's going to happen next, and that everyone's different. I learned a few things that worked for me, but there are no guarantees that they'll work for anyone else.

1. *Prepare to clear out your life.* You never know what will go away. I was lucky that most of what I lost was a marriage, a house, and a bunch of money, but even there, we had a pretty amicable divorce

and my daughter came around in a couple of years, and we never stopped talking to each other.

With my mother, I was fortunate – at least in this case – to have had a major bike accident a month before I told her face to face, and she told me that she was just happy that I was still alive. The older of my two sisters, who I thought would be OK with it, questioned me like the second-wave feminist that she is (and that I have considered myself to be, too): 'If gender doesn't matter, why do you want to change yours?' This is a real question that I think transgender people should be able to answer. We might have always felt that we were the other gender, but I don't think that one's idea of the gender in which one is not living can be as complete as if one had lived one's entire life in that gender. Saying otherwise is classic mansplaining. That doesn't mean that you *can't* figure out what it means to you to be a woman and why it is so important to change, but it does mean that you should think about it. Having the half of the population which you are joining on your side is very powerful!

2. *Take as much time as you can.* I worked on my voice and general appearance (short of surgery and medication) to be more passably female, for several years. I even had my hair cut to a shorter feminine style just so I'd look different. You're not going to be perceived the same way by others after you transition. Figure out how you want them to think of you. Do you really want to continue to be the girly girl that you tried to be after you realized what gender you really were? It takes time to become a woman! It helps to have a few role-models in your life who have similar styles to what you think would be your own. In mid-transition, I showed up at my best female friend's house – having friends of

your destination gender is fantastic if you can find them, and I didn't expect to – for a party, and when she answered the door, we fell down laughing because we were quite unexpectedly both wearing the same skirt. She changed.

I tried to tell people one-on-one as much as I could, in person if possible, over the six months before I went full-time (April to November 2011). I had some pretty good photographs by then that could convince people that this person that they always thought of as masculine already passed as a woman. When I showed my somewhat conservative Midwestern American 80-year-old aunt, she told me that I should get highlights in my hair, and our friendship continued, despite that fact that I am so far happy with how my hair looks: it does nicely reflect sunlight.

3. *Do volunteer work!* I have been a bicycle and open-space activist for decades, and I transitioned in those communities before I did at work or at home. While there is tons of advice online and in books about transitioning in the workplace and with your family, I couldn't find anything about changing one's gender in a volunteer community. I served on several boards and had a reputation as someone who was always contributing to efforts to change the world in a positive direction. I took the occasion of a board diversity and inclusion training workshop to tell one executive director. Before the event, just in case it came up (and in 2009, gender identity did not), I emailed her an explanatory message I had carefully worked out with my psychotherapist-then-spouse, and she immediately called me back. 'You're not going to leave, are you?' she asked. After assuring her that I wouldn't, my life in that group gradually changed, and she changed my name on the organization letterhead well before it was legally changed.

The other board members were congratulatory, which took me by surprise then, but has been a recurring experience. Here is the letter I wrote:

> I'm looking forward to tomorrow's day of diversity training because I think the environmental movement needs to look like the country as a whole, and we don't, though I think **** has done a great job in trying to include its community. I may not seem to be the most 'diverse' person on the board, but I thought that on the eve of our meeting I should tell you that I am more so than it seems. I am a member of the T part of LGBT, a male to female transgendered person, that is, I identify more as a woman than as a man, a condition sometimes known as gender identity disorder or gender dysphoria. This is an issue which I have been struggling with for most of my life, and my future direction is unclear. Recently, it has been having more of an effect on my life and it seems like this is an appropriate time to make important people in my life aware of it. I know that LGBT diversity has not been a major issue in the environmental movement and may not be on our agenda Saturday, but as our community gains acceptance for our very existence, we have energy which can be devoted to other causes such as open space. In my case, being able to be myself in the world is freeing me from constraints which have held me back from committing more of myself. I continue to believe in the mission of **** and will work to further our shared goals. If you have any questions, feel free to call or email me. If it is appropriate as part of our session this weekend, I am willing to say something to the group about gender identity. [male name here]

In my bicycle world, I received a lifetime activism award three months after I went full-time. Over half the audience wondered why this woman that they had never seen before was getting such an award, but enough people knew and told the people sitting around them that I ended up getting a standing ovation from all 500 people in the room – about the most affirming thing that has ever happened to me.

4. *I no longer had this giant secret at the center of my life!* All of a sudden, I could be open about who I am. Despite early ideas about making big changes in my life and profession, I realized that my past was a big help in moving into a differently gendered future. I pretty much held onto everything I had ever done, professionally and otherwise. This meant that if they investigated (just by following links on my website) people would know that I had not always been the same gender. It took me a few years before transitioning to get comfortable with this. Over time, I've learned to talk about my past in a gender-free way, even with people who know that I'm trans, so that no one has to face the cognitive dissonance of someone having lived in two genders in every conversation that involves past events which aren't gender-relevant.

5. *I used the opportunity of becoming an outwardly different person (even if feeling the same inside) to work on my rough edges.* For a few years, I had one therapist to help me deal with gender issues and another to help me figure out the other things which were limiting my life and effectiveness. Even though I haven't fixed myself, I understand more about myself than my gender, and I think that has helped me to be a better friend and colleague.

6. *Don't take yourself too seriously!* If you get upset every time someone misgenders you, you will be perpetually angry. I'm fortunate to have always been mostly passable as either gender (maybe less so as male these days), so there has always been some uncertainty from other people. I have decided that anyone who has known me over ten years gets a lifetime pass on getting my pronouns wrong, as long as it's not purposefully nasty. I'll correct them every time, though sometimes just with a look. And people that knew me before for less time before get nicely corrected, and are usually extremely apologetic.

Jessica Mink

Lauren Harries

....

Lauren Harries is a British TV personality who became a media sensation as a child – dubbed a child prodigy and Britain's youngest tycoon – even being invited to appear on *Oprah*. At the age of 22 she transitioned, making headlines again, and was invited back on *Oprah*. Most recently, she was on *Celebrity Big Brother*, where she won over the hearts of the British nation, making it to the final and finishing in third place.

....

I Am

I never thought I was a boy, as a child I was full of joy.

Teachers called me pansy, but I didn't mind, I was blissfully unaware they were being unkind.

I was happy being applauded on TV, that applause was enough for me.

At the age of 12, I left school and found, how happy I was just looking around.

*I chose my own books, learnt why we were
here, I had no troubles and I had no fear.*

*Then puberty came and I was in a mire, I began
to wonder and I began to enquire.*

*On my 18th birthday I cried all day, I didn't
fancy girls and I was not gay.*

*I went to a club with an acquaintance one week,
but in that club they thought me a freak.*

*Heterosexual men were the ones for me, but I
was just James and they could not see.*

*When my dream came true and my body complete, I
thanked the universe for being so sweet.*

*Finally my body had caught up with my mind, the
universe had listened and was being kind.*

*Women's clothing was chosen by me, I
tried to look the best I could be.*

After 22 years I dressed like a girl, I walked the town in a whirl.

*My agent Max Clifford said 'Tell the press', and
at the time I was under duress.*

*My operation had put my family in debt, that
was one of my biggest regrets.*

*I knew I'd make money on TV and then
the debt would be settled by me.*

*I ranted in the papers and went on TV, I was
revealed as Lauren for all to see.*

Life on the street became insane, passers-by would call me names.

*Tranny, weirdo, shirt-lifter freak, but I didn't
allow them to make me weak.*

*Some called insults as their cars passed by, I would
try to be strong, I would try not to cry.*

*If relatives saw me they'd turn in fright, how
could they be seen with such a sight.*

*Some cousins took me out to eat, but they
criticised me from head to feet.*

*They did not like to be seen with what they thought was a
freak, they were too insecure, they were just too weak.*

*I was wearing a wig because my hair was too
short, when a girl pulled it off just for sport.*

*Bigots would throw bricks into our space, when we
answered the door the bullies would race.*

*Once the bigots broke in when I was alone, before
help arrived they had broken my cheek bone.*

*They left my face weak, prone to swelling and pain, my
dad caught one and we weren't bothered again.*

*My publicity spread as far as Dubai, while I
was there a man spat in my eye.*

*But those who love me kept me strong, they
knew the others were so very wrong.*

*Automatically a woman ordered me out of the
gym, for me to be in the ladies was such a sin.*

Then I went on CBB and Lauren was there for all to see. Somehow folk began to understand, someone even asked to hold my hand.

Most understood how I tick, that I am not weird, that I am not sick.

I am just the woman I was born to be, my soul is bare for all to see, but attraction in men I don't evoke, some don't see a girl, they see a bloke.

I'd like to say I don't give a damn, that men care who I am, but sometimes for love I yearn from a man who takes time to learn.

A man who will give me a sexy stare, a man who is strong and doesn't care.

A man who will hold my hand and walk, a man who understands, a man who could talk.

I am Lauren who I think is great, but I will postpone finding a mate, although I am caring pretty and kind, I have other things on my mind.

I will always be remembered and on TV, because that is where I am meant to be.

Some TV producers think I'm great, other TV producers are afraid and get in a state, we must make an impact on this world, we must keep prejudice unfurled.

We will make folk loving and good, by teaching them to love as they should.

Why should we cast judgement on our peers, we have the same problems, we have the same fears.

*We're on the same journey, we share the same
fight, to judge someone else we have no right.*

*Whether transgender, gay or black, don't
talk about folk behind their back.*

*Don't babble and bicker and stare and hate, if you
understood that person, they could be your soul mate.*

*Our souls are actually all the same, so
please don't hate, it's such a shame.*

*Thank you for taking the time to listen, if I've
done my job your eyes will aglisten.*

Lauren Harries

Stu Rasmussen

....

Stu Rasmussen is an American politician who became the nation's first openly transgender mayor when elected as the mayor of Silverton, Oregon in November 2008. Stu was also elected a member of the city council three times. In 2013 a musical about Stu's life and career, *Stu for Silverton*, premiered at Seattle's Intiman theatre.

....

To my trans sisters,

I hope you are enjoying your travels on the gender spectrum. Here's some stuff I learned the hard way:

- First of all – be yourself – nobody is better at it than you.
- And the corollary: Do not apologize for being yourself.
- No, everyone is *not* looking at you – they're mostly engaged in their own lives and only rarely venture outside their cocoons.
- Have a pair of flats available.
- 'Tomorrow' is not as good as 'today' for getting something done.

- If you're changing names, pick one with the same initials.
- The spectrum of shoes runs from 'stylish' to 'comfortable'.
- You cannot be in two places at once.
- Brassiere sizing is an arcane art, not a science.
- If you fall while wearing heels (and you will), try to do it gracefully and not break a nail.
- Breast augmentation is worth every penny.
- Spandex is probably not your friend.
- Cultivate good friends – and be one yourself.
- Life is short. Heels shouldn't be.
- A dream without a plan is just a wish.
- Have fun and stay pretty!

Stu

Natalie van Gogh

....

Natalie van Gogh is a Dutch professional racing cyclist and one of the most notable professional transgender sportspeople in the world. In 2006 she began riding in local competitions, and later that year competed at a national level with impressive results, causing a stir the media. In 2007 she competed with a regional elite women's team at the highest national level and progressed to an international level in 2011, where she has since competed in international races such as the UCI of Gent-Wevelgem, Ronde van Overijssel and GP Maarten Wynants (winning seventh, second and first place, respectively).

....

To my trans sisters,

Well, let's be real about transitioning. You will face stress over whether you can convince the gender clinic that transitioning is what is best for you. You will face the awkward period when you start transitioning. You will face the pain of the hair removal and surgeries. And afterwards it will always be something you will carry with you no matter how 'passable' you are.

But you know what, it's nothing compared to the continuous feeling that something is 'off'; that life feels like your right shoe is on your left foot and vice versa; you can put one foot in front of the other but it never feels like walking; the nagging voice in the back of your head which keeps on playing that tune 'What if...?', 'Why am I not...?'; the feeling that life sucks; the dreams at night; the unanswered prayers when going to bed. It puts a stress on you that will only build when you get older, to the point where you start to withdraw, isolate yourself or do stupid things.

And then you decide to transition and that freaking voice inside your head stops. It's silent, almost creepily silent. So, this is what most (cis) people experience: the nothing, the absolute freedom to think about 'normal' things (define what is normal?). There is time in your thoughts to start to feel the urge to do stuff, to live! Living life begins to feel normal, you start walking, venturing out, opening the world.

You know, sis, there is something else that held me back, making me believe that transitioning wasn't for me. It was the stupid social stigma that is on girls/women/transwomen. I am so happy to see that this is slowly disappearing. The only transwomen I was able to see as an example when I was a child were either ultra femme Barbies, hookers or drag queens and I couldn't identify with any of them. I was (and still am) this geeky tomboy who liked the endorphins of sport. For years I struggled with the fact that I thought transitioning wasn't for me because I wasn't like those trans girls who cried in the toy store to get a Barbie (I wanted a BMX bike) and who cried over not getting that princess dress (I'd rather have that Atari PC). It was only when I got older (when I was 25) that I met the (trans) girls I did identify with. It opened my eyes to the fact that my personality does not define my gender, nor the other way around.

I also want to share a piece of advice. So often I see that the transition becomes someone's full focus. They have nothing else to focus on but that single aspect. Don't do that! Look at transition as something that is part of your normal daily life, but don't let it *become* life. Go to work, go to school, find a hobby, do volunteer work, meet and make friends. Just keep yourself busy with all kinds of stuff outside of your house. It makes transitioning easier. Transitioning takes time, it takes patience, and being social makes it easier to integrate yourself into society and overcome those anxieties when you venture out into the world for the first time.

Just remember, you have the right to do anything you want. I began living by this rule when I started transitioning. Being transgendered has not stopped me doing what I want. When the bike racing bug hit me and I decided that I wanted to race, it did occur to me that it could lead to confrontations (as it did for Michelle Dumaresq) – and it did as soon as I started to become a real competitor for the prize money – but I just stuck my head down and continued as I firmly believe that I have the right to do what I love. And so should you.

With love,

Natalie

Hannah Phillips

....

Seventeen-year-old Hannah Phillips is a public speaker and activist. She uses her YouTube channel to educate people around trans issues and also travels around the UK giving talks on the subject and working with policy-makers to make their institutions more trans inclusive. This includes her work with NHS CAMHS (Child and Adolescent Mental Health Services) and her work on the Gender Recognition Act. Hannah has been awarded two Princess Diana Awards for her activism. She also has advanced knowledge of computers and has developed eLearning software for Praxis.

....

To my trans sisters,

On 1 January 2017, I pledged to my YouTube audience that I would make a video every day. This was for no other reason than to show the world what life is like for a transgender teen. How it is no different to the life of a cisgender person, apart from going through the processes which a transgender person takes to become who they are on the inside.

As I write this, I have produced over 134 videos this year, which is more videos than there have been days. Fifty-three of them are transgender topic-related and 66 of them are videos of my day-to-day life. My journey over the next few months will be taking a different turn. I will be starting oestrogen (the female hormone) to become who I need to be; this will affect me and the videos I create.

Filmmaking was a passion of mine before and after I started to transition. For me, to transition doesn't mean you are becoming someone else; it means you are becoming who you are. And at the end of the day, being who you are is the best sort of self-love you can give yourself. Be you, be true and stay real!

Hannah Phillips

Joan Roughgarden

Joan Roughgarden, PhD, is an ecologist and evolutionary biologist who has published more than 180 papers and 8 books, including *Evolution's Rainbow* (2004), which won the 2005 Stonewall Prize for non-fiction from the American Library Association. She is best known for her work on theistic evolutionism and her critical studies of Charles Darwin's theory of sexual selection. She gained her doctorate in biology from Harvard University in 1971 and has taught at Stanford University since 1972 as Professor of Biology and Geophysics, transitioning in 1998. In 1992 Joan founded and directed the Earth Systems Program for which she received the Dinkelspiel Award for service to undergraduate education.

....

To my trans sisters,

Just a brief note here from your Auntie Joan. I transitioned nearly 20 years ago. Lots of changes since then, but, hey, lots the same too.

So, a big issue back then was to get the T added to LGB. Organizations from universities to the caucuses of political parties were just becoming aware of trans folks and were mulling whether to include us. I remember explicitly thanking the gay caucus of the California Democratic Party for adding the T to their name – they appreciated being thanked, and even applauded. Today, trans people are generally included as part of the LGBT community, despite the tensions that remain and sometimes surface.

The other big issue was getting out from under the thumb of the therapists. They wanted, and many still want, to control our identity. It was hard to speak at a forum without the organizers requiring a therapist to be present to authenticate whatever we said. We lacked standing to have our own voice recognized as authoritative about our own experience. This is better now. Still, we're always fighting a rear guard battle against therapists who want to discredit anything we say as nothing but propaganda, and who value their own theories about who we are more than they value our own testimonials about who we actually are.

The strained relation between trans folks and therapists remains. Therapists make a living from us as their clients, or patients as they would prefer to call us. They have every incentive to pathologize us because that guarantees their income stream. The problem for us is to avoid self-pathologizing. If you really think there is something the matter with you, well, you're wrong. Read my stuff about gender in biology and across different cultures. We're eternal and global. The trans people who support retaining us in the American Psychiatric Association's *Diagnostic and Statistical Manual* (*DSM*), so they can get medical insurance benefits, are thinking short term. After all, transition does end. A *DSM* diagnosis can, and will, be used against us after transition.

Going forward, here's my advice. First, don't wait. If you know you're trans, get off your ass and do your transition. Hanging out in the wings, doing a half-and-half thing, will destroy you and the ones who love you. Face up to reality, that's what we women do. Second, decide what kind of woman you are. Are you a professional woman? Are you a wife, a mother? Are you an artist, a scientist, an engineer, a musician, a writer, a soldier, a park ranger, a politician, a disk jockey, a whatever? And watch out for the glam thing. Not many women are actresses or fashion models. You probably aren't either, so dress appropriately. Third, aim high. Think long term. Make a life and live it.

Sincerely,

Joan

Becky Allison

....

Cardiologist Becky Allison has served as President of the Gay and Lesbian Medical Association (GLMA): Health Professionals Advancing LGBT Equality, as Chair of the American Medical Association's Advisory Committee on Gay, Lesbian, Bisexual and Transgender Issues and as a board member of the World Professional Association for Transgender Health. She has also maintained the website drbecky.com, a resource site for the trans community providing medical, legal and spiritual advice to those at the start of their transition. *Phoenix* magazine named her one of the 'top doctors' in 2006, 2007 and 2008.

....

To my (older) trans sisters,

So I understand you're a little bit older – maybe we might even say 'middle age' – is that right? I hear you! That's my story too!

And you've been trying so hard, for years, NOT to face this gender conflict. Before matters got so intense, you worked hard and made a nice life – as a guy. Job? Family? You had a lot to lose. But the conflict didn't go away – it never does – and one day you knew you had to face your truth: you are going to live the rest of your life as the woman, you know you are. Congratulations! It took strength and courage to get to this point.

Now what?

Before you 'go public', there's so much planning to do. I'm assuming you want to go ahead with a full transition. More about that in a minute. I'm old school – I still think a therapist is so helpful for a successful transition, then a healthcare provider for medications, and an electrologist for, well, electrology, which is important for living and working in the real world. The good news is that, being a little older, you have a job and probably can afford most of this.

If you've already established yourself in a career, you want to continue in that career if at all possible. Do you work for a large company with a Human Resources department? It's likely they have done this before. They can help you with a timetable, and together you can decide when the time is right to 'come out' to your co-workers. Then you can think about changing your name on your birth certificate, diplomas and legal documents. Change your gender marker when you can. It's time-consuming but worth the effort.

Do you have a family? You have to do right by your family. They didn't sign up for this adventure. If your spouse is a special person, and she remains with you through transition, you are fortunate beyond words. That may not happen. Try to remain friends. Above all, if you have children, remain a part of their lives and let them know you will still love them, no matter what. Don't abandon your loved ones if at all possible.

What about surgery? Most people I hear from still want surgery. Some can't have it for medical reasons, and some can't afford it. But gender reassignment surgery (GRS) is important for most of us. If possible, facial feminization and tracheal shave make a great difference in blending in. You can have a good life and a successful transition without them, but it's good to know you have all those options.

You can do this, sis. You have a lot of support. Most cities have in-person support groups. There's always online support from Facebook and various mailing lists. Others are going through the same process. Before long, you will be the one offering advice to them! And the day will come when you look back and say, 'This was the hardest thing I have ever done. AND I DID IT.'

We are all cheering you on.

Love,

Becky Allison

Bionka Simone

....

Bionka Simone is the star of popular TV show *Transcendent*, a docu-series that follows the lives of five American transgender women. The show, now in its second season, was nominated for a GLAAD Award. Bionka spoke on the show about the struggles facing trans people in America today, shedding light on issues such as bullying in schools, family rejection and youth homelessness. She went on to win the prestigious Miss Gay United States pageant in 2016.

....

To my trans sisters,

Going through this trans-girl journey isn't going to be smooth. It might break you down and make you ask yourself 'Why am I going through with this?' But your heart is gonna tell you that no matter what, you're not complete... Well, sista, I'm here to tell you that only the strong survive and that you are a survivor, so hold your head up and smile, my child! As trans people we are leaders, and together or apart we are a force to be reckoned with. Hold your head up with pride.

xo

Your sister, Bionka Simone

Maria Clara Spinelli

....

Maria Clara Spinelli is a Brazilian actress who came to prominence after starring in the film *Quanto Dura o Amor?*, for which she won the Best Actress award in the Paulínia Film Festival, the Brazilian Film Festival and the Monaco Charity Film Festival. She was also nominated for Best Actress in the VI FIESP/SESI-SP Award of Cinema Paulista. In 2013, she starred in the popular telenovela *Salve Jorge*, in which she played the character Anita, and in 2016, she starred in the popular series *Supermax*, on TV Globo, the biggest TV network in South America.

....

To my trans sisters,

If you are reading this letter, I believe you are on the right path, for you have already discovered who you are; a woman... And this is the most important thing! And to this woman, I want to say a few words.

First of all, love yourself. Know that you are perfect in your heart, and the body is just matter which can be shaped, like clay.

The world is not ready for us yet... Because we are the future! The freedom to choose and to shape our destinies and our bodies is in our hands. We are creators and creatures at the same time. We have given birth to ourselves. Life has given us this gift. Perhaps we are not as beloved as other people, since we cause fear and revolt in those who cannot choose their own destiny, as we do. But we can love a lot! And I've discovered, in the end, that giving love is much greater than receiving it.

Yes, it is a long and arduous journey, but it is possible to get through it with dignity, beauty and love.

With my best feelings,

Maria Clara Spinelli

Drew-Ashlyn Cunningham

....

Drew-Ashlyn Cunningham starred on Channel 4's groundbreaking *My Transsexual Summer* in 2011. After the show she used her platform and popularity for good, travelling around the country to give talks at schools, colleges and universities to educate people about trans issues. She continues to educate people, now using her popular YouTube channel where she has documented her transition and showcases her work as a make-up artist.

....

To my trans sisters,

How are you all?! Well, I'm feeling fantastic. So where do I start, ay, hmmm, let's see... Well first off, I want to say if you're not feeling fantastic, that's OK, and do you know why? Because I was in the same position, too. So I wanted to give you some insight about me and maybe you'll be able to draw some advice from what I've said, otherwise I'm just babbling on, ain't I?

I was born Andrew Colin James Cunningham in a little place called Aldershot here in the UK. I know, posh right, haha. My mum is loud, proud and full of life and my dad was always away in the army so I never got to see him much. I grew up with two older sisters. One was a bubbly, silly, live-for-the-moment kinda girl and the other was a serious bookworm, who, yes, I used to argue with a lot...like a lot.

I guess being in an all-female environment was the best thing ever, as I got to be myself. I was able to play with dolls and play dress-up; and when the Spice Girls came out, I got to be sporty! How cool is that.

I never understood why I was different but, then again, I never got the opportunity to question it because my home life was so open that to me I was normal to my family. It wasn't until I got older and was faced with depression, bullying, being beaten up behind the gates at school and feeling like I was the only one who fancied the guys and wanted to dress like the girls that I really started to question who I was and who I am.

I tried to be a super macho boy, by dressing as a skater kid and training as a wrestler! I faced being called gay on a daily basis and just decided to take it. As time went on I started battling my depression and researching online what was wrong with me. At first I just assumed I was gay because I knew that I was attracted to men (Randy Orton, call me). It wasn't until I had seen an interview on YouTube with the plastic fantastic Amanda Lepore that by penny dropped. I was mesmerized. The idea that this woman was once male stunned me. This was it, I knew who I was. I could relate to someone finally. I didn't feel like an alien anymore. I knew I wanted to be a woman and I finally had an answer to who I was and why I felt like this. Coming out was the hardest thing, so I dragged it out for as long as I could. I would only dress up at night, stealing my sister's clothes and wearing my mum's make-up while she was working a night shift at the nursing home. I felt free and alive. I was about 17 at this point, so I'd be online chatting to guys, seeking approval from them, seeing if they thought I looked like a woman or not. I'd be up all night, then I'd go get undressed, wash the face I'd created with my mum's make-up and go to bed and sleep through the day.

My college grades were getting low, and I was constantly having letters sent home to my mum saying I hadn't been for almost a month! My mum went mad and told me I had to get help. She couldn't stand seeing me down, but this is the thing, I was only down when I was dressed as Andrew. I was alive when I could be my true self – the girl I should have been born as. There was a night that would change everything. My mum had gone to see a doctor that day and told him how I was behaving, saying I wasn't eating and I was self-harming, and saying she had seen pictures of me in my diary that I had drawn where I appeared as a girl. He mentioned that it sounded like I was transgender. My mum cried in relief. Her and my sister tried to think of a way for me to come out and open up so they didn't have to see me down anymore. They burst into my room and randomly asked if I'd taken my sister's pill. I woke up feeling groggy and answered, 'WTF, no!' They then went on to ask if I was gay, if I wanted to be a drag queen and then it came to the last question: 'Do you want to be a girl?' I just cried and cried and OMG there was just snot everywhere. I didn't even know I could produce that much snot. We laughed and cried some more. In the end I knew my family would be OK because of how open they are. Just the idea of coming out was terrifying; all them years of being depressed was for nothing. If I'd known then what I know now, I'd have come out sooner.

As time's gone on, I've learnt to love myself more and more and to not be afraid. All my life I've been scared to take chances, like not coming out sooner or not having facial surgery for the fear of being in debt. Since then, I've become a much happier person and I try not to question things and just go for it. I went on to be a barmaid, a Lady Gaga impersonator, and then starred in Channel 4's *My Transsexual Summer*. Now I work for an amazing make-up company, Illamasqua, and I've even been given the title of the first transgender wrestler in the UK.

So, 'Who am I?' you wonder.

I'm simply Drew-Ashlyn Cunningham – more than a blonde and more than a label. My advice that I always tell people is this: we're all soft and pink on the inside; if you're not being yourself, then what's the point in being you.

xox

Drew-Ashlyn Cunningham

Paula Coffer

....

Paula Coffer is a war veteran, with over 24 years of service. She served in the US Navy from 1970 to 1974 during the Vietnam War, and then as a second lieutenant in the US Army Finance Corps from 1977 to 1994. After her service in the US Army she authored *Terezon: A Meditative Guide for Inner Strength* and became an accomplished gender diversity lecturer at universities throughout the Midwest. In 2000 she was named in Pinnacle's *Who's Who in American Business*. Paula shared her life story in her memoir *Sandbox to Sandbox*, and shared the story of her time in Afghanistan in her *Afghan Journals* trilogy.

....

To my trans sisters,

What an opportunity this is. A chance for me to have a 'do over' or to 'travel back in time'. The basic question of what I would do differently in transitioning, now that I have lived my life as Paula for the past 22 years, is a most interesting concept.

There is a tremendous amount of guidance available on the Internet and through social groups to inform a person considering transition. Guidance is available for changing your name and gender markers on birth certificates, driver's licenses, and military discharge documents. Guidance is available for locating trans-friendly endocrinologists and physicians. Guidance is even available on how to modify your voice, do your nails, select clothing and apply make-up. There are even Facebook pages where a transitioning individual posts daily their ongoing experiences interacting with family, clients and the public in general.

What I don't see though is anything indicating the emotional and psychological issues that are encountered. I don't see the reality for employment being addressed. I don't see where guidance is provided for how to handle uncomfortable situations.

I transitioned before there was an Internet and the guide for 'how to transition' did not exist. That doesn't matter though. The things about transition that really count are you and how you perceive life in general. Your attitude can make all the difference in the world. I like to say, 'Walk in confidence', confidence that you are in the right place at the right time, doing the right thing. More on confidence later.

I recall an incident early in my transition where a girlfriend and I were at a gas station. We went in together and the young man's reaction to us was rather obvious. It was early evening and we were dressed for a social event. He must have found us somewhat comical, and while he wasn't rude, he wasn't a 'friend' either. My friend immediately left and returned to the car, but I took the opportunity to try and educate the young man. I chose to educate him on providing great customer service rather than scold him on not being nice to a transwoman. I think this approach works because I'm not asking for anything special. I don't feel I deserve a special status; I just want to be treated like a valued customer, respected as a person. Of course my friend was decimated by the encounter and internalized the rejection she felt by 'not passing'. This pretty much ruined her evening. Don't let other people's opinion or attitude affect your feelings about yourself and your self-esteem!

Another incident occurred during one of our monthly support group meetings, where we would all go to Applebee's for dinner on a Saturday night. We had arrived early, to ensure we had seating, and occupied several of the window booths. I noticed a few of the girls getting anxious. They were looking around the restaurant and it looked like they were ready to bolt out the door at any minute. I asked what was wrong. 'Just look at these people laughing at us,' one girl said. I looked around and, sure enough, there were people in the restaurant that were laughing, joking around with each other and looking out the windows – probably people-watching as it was that part of town. I turned around to the girls and asked them why they would think that these people's experience tonight had anything to do with them. I asked why they thought everything was about them. You can't always have your emotions and fears on your sleeve. Let these things go and realize that you are not that important to others that are out to have a good time. Oh, certainly, there are others that will momentarily look at you and make a remark to their companion, but for the most part I don't believe people care about you or your enjoyment; rather they are there for their own enjoyment. As we observed these other restaurant patrons, it became obvious that they were wrapped up in their own activities and not involved in making fun of us. The girls finally settled down and began to enjoy a night out on the town, being among others with a common goal of being ourselves.

Take on an attitude of 'don't care'. Don't care what other people say. Prior to transition I had to care what people thought of me. I was an army officer, father and husband living a dual life. After I transitioned and struggled through the physical and environmental changes, I finally realized that it didn't matter what others thought of me. The only thing that mattered was how I felt about myself and I adapted an attitude of 'I don't care.' With an 'I don't care' attitude came the confidence to forge into the world, facing my challenges in a much more positive way.

Don't care that you are not where you want to be yet. Transition takes time. Don't be disappointed with your progress; rather look at how far you have come, much like counting your blessings. Don't care also means that everything is not about you. When you notice that someone is laughing or pointing in your general direction, this doesn't mean it is about you. You truly are not that important to others and the joke told or item pointed out is probably not you, just your dysphoria or paranoia. Along these same lines, don't get upset when 'sir' or 'him' is used. Remember that you are the sensitive one and people have known you for years as a male. They will modify their usage in time. Be patient, but also be consistent in gently reminding others with a nice 'her' or 'ma'am'.

This is a journey and the destination is only a short-term goal. You will continue to set new goals and have new aspirations as you travel down this path. Life is a journey! I so remember all the little things that brought me so much concern and fear. Going into the Driver's License Bureau to have my driver's license changed was one of those events. For days before I went in I would imagine the worst of scenarios. I feared being embarrassed or being insulted or being disrespected and made fun of. I was as nervous as a cat on a hot tin roof to enter that building. Of course all my fears and concerns were unfounded and I received my new driver's license with the correct name and gender and photo with no problem at all. No one made fun of me or paid any special attention to me. This event, like so many others, had such a strong emotional build-up, but once it was over, it was totally anticlimactic. So while you may feel like this might be the end of your world, it is just another day; and after it has passed, you won't give it another thought. Walk in confidence into the world, expecting the greatest of outcomes and accepting nothing less!

One of the primary pieces of advice I have for you is to blend in. Be a part of the normal everyday society that we live in. Don't be that person that has to make a statement by being so 'out there' in garish clothing, make-up, etc., always the center of attention. My success has been achieved by just being one of the girls. I've lived in a 'don't ask, don't tell' world, but if asked I always tell everything. To me this means that I don't advertise that I'm a transwoman but I don't hide it either. When confronted, I don't get embarrassed; I just answer honestly and work with the person to help them understand what a transwoman is – just another spiritual being having a human experience! There have been very few people that have ever asked me though. I'm sure they knew I was a transwoman but it must not have mattered.

Be prepared for transition with your eyes wide open. There is a period where you are just ugly! Electrolysis is an emotional event! Embarrassment as you let the hair grow for a day or so before your appointment. Then your face is red afterward as you travel home or back to work. As you begin taking hormones, your emotions take you through puberty all over again. You will have the desire to dress in age-inappropriate attire as you begin experimenting with your new-found feelings. Remember that you don't live in a fantasy world and be practical more than showy. Don't waste your money on clothing or accessories that you won't wear more than once or twice. Don't get frustrated with the pace your body is changing with the hormones as we all develop differently. Don't attempt to self-medicate yourself. I did and because of the size of the dosage I became depressed and really did some stupid things. Also don't attempt self-surgery. I did and was very fortunate that I didn't develop any complications.

Accepting yourself isn't as easy as you may think. For me, I lost everything: career, family relationships, home, friends. I would think I could go back and make everything OK, but that would or could never happen. Once this big cat was out of the bag, no bag would ever hold it again. Each time I considered giving up and getting out of transition I would sit back and tell myself, 'Being here is my choice. Suck it up and make the very best of the situation and get through this event.' There have been times when I cried for what I've lost. But then I have to reflect that it isn't necessarily me that has lost anything. The people that I thought loved me didn't love me enough to let me grow and help me to be happy. For me it was pretty much a life-or-death situation. Had I not transitioned, I would have committed suicide as I was that miserable living the dual existence where neither was anywhere near happy.

You have to realistic about employment. Let's face it, if you are 6 feet 5 inches tall with football shoulders you probably won't do well in the retail industry selling cosmetics. This may in fact be your dream job and what you have always aspired to be. But the chances are you'll never succeed in this position, so set your sights differently. If you still want to work in the retail industry – in, say, some major department store – then start at whatever position you can acquire. Perhaps you start as a warehouse worker or office worker and spend your time earning the respect of your fellow workers while observing the women you wish to emulate. I have started at the bottom or near bottom with a couple of my opportunities and then worked my way up to where I wanted to be. This allowed my co-workers to become familiar with me and accept me for the skills and talents I brought to the workplace. It does a transperson no good to transition and then not be able to support themselves and fulfill their obligations to their children/family. If I had near unlimited funds, I would create a transition center where employment and life skills are taught to help the person transitioning better cope with their new life. Perhaps I'll win the lottery one day and fulfill a business plan I created in 1989 where persons transitioning lived, studied and worked until they could move on in the world and succeed.

Here are three instances where having confidence created support from others:

When I interviewed with the National Credit Union Administration in 2000 for a position as a Federal Examiner, one of the interviewers commented that my resume listed the US Navy and service aboard the USS *Oriskany*. He said that he served aboard the USS *Ranger* during this same period and he didn't remember women being aboard ship. I responded, 'You'd be surprised, we were everywhere.' Nothing more was said and I was hired for the position, with the management knowing I was a transwoman.

In 2004 I was teaching at the International Business College when a group of my accounting students googled me and discovered that I was a transwoman. The parents of one of the students approached the school administrators and complained that they didn't want their daughter being taught by me. This was the first time the Director of Education had an indication that I was a transwoman. I was fully supported by all the administrators and the parents were told that they should withdraw their daughter if there was an issue with me being the instructor as I was the best

Department Head and instructor that they had ever had for the accounting program. As a side note, this girl came to my office each day for tutoring until her parents forced her to stop. She at least valued my teaching skills.

In 2007 I worked as the Director of Finance and Administration at a Job Corps Center. My IT manager googled me and learned that I am a transwoman. He began spreading the news without confronting me. I was again supported by the Center Director and Corporate Headquarters. The Corporate Director of Human Resources came to discuss this with him. He received a counseling, while I received an apology.

The point in me sharing these three events is that it is OK that you are seen as a transwoman. You don't have to be total stealth and in the closet. You can live your life openly doing the kind of work you want to do by walking in confidence.

One more instance I wish to relate is from 2014. My position was with the State Department in Kabul, Afghanistan. My primary function was to advise the Deputy Commanding General on financial strategy and policies with regard to the United Nations and the Afghanistan Police Ministry. I briefed generals, ambassadors and senior staff for Resource Management as part of my duties. Not only was I well respected for what I could contribute to the NATO forces, but I was well received by the Afghanistan police generals and deputy ministers that I dealt with. Walk in confidence!

Take the high road every time! I don't argue with people. If someone is nasty, I walk away as it just isn't worth it to talk with someone who already dislikes or despises you. I let the situation go and don't even think about it anymore, because the more energy you give it, the more it grows and it only affects you. The other person has already let it go and moved on to other things.

A hater is a hater and you can't bring love into their hearts. Look forward to what can be and don't dwell on what could've been or was. I find that being positive with a can-do attitude toward what is possible and keeping a sense of strength about myself allows me to walk in confidence. Being confident is a gift. To me, being confident means that I'm not showing that I might be afraid – afraid of failure, afraid of rejection, afraid of being laughed at, afraid of not being me. I walk in confidence knowing that I'm a spiritual being having a human experience. The only way this experience is going to work out is if I'm committed to making this the best day possible. So, if I choose to live this day, then I must choose to make it the best day ever. I have to walk in confidence as a role model to younger transpeople. I have to walk in confidence as a parent where my children can respect me for staying the course and living the life I have chosen to live. While I truly feel that being a transperson is an 'uninvited dilemma', I also believe that we have a choice in how we present ourselves. For me, I presented as male for 41 years before presenting as a female for the last 23 years.

Paula Coffer

Nikki Exotika

....

Nikki Exotika is a singer and media personality who came to prominence on *Transtasia*, a documentary that followed contestants competing for the title of 'The World's Most Beautiful Transsexual'. After the show, she launched her music career, releasing an array of pop and dance anthems such as 'Young, Wild and Free', 'All Lined Up' and 'Secret Girl'. Nikki is also the mastermind behind America's first trans girl group, The Secret Girls.

....

To my trans sisters,

PLEASE DONT PUSSY STUNT!!!

Pussy stuntin' is when a trans woman doesn't tell her T to a man she is being sexually active with. Things can go horribly wrong and you can end up hurt, in the hospital, or dead!

I'm going to tell you my story...

This was a time after I had my sex reassignment surgery (SRS) – maybe two years after – and I was living my life stealth, working as a go-go dancer at dance clubs in New York City. I met a really handsome man that happened to be a police officer in Queens, New York. We dated for a few weeks, went on many dates and had lots of great conversation and fun together. We obviously made love too – which was so amazing. He even introduced me to his entire family and they all loved me. The day he told me that he loved me, I was in shock I wasn't really expecting him to say that so soon; it didn't feel right because he didn't know the real me. I said to him but how do you know that you love me? He said because I just do. He then said, 'Why would you ask that?' I tried to break the ice and started the conversation about kids and having a child that was either born gay or different and he said, 'What do you mean by different?' And I said, 'What if our child was born transgender?' He said he didn't know because he'd never been in a situation like that before, so I just blurted it out: 'What if I was born different or transgender?!' He looked at me with shock, horror, confusion and disgust in his eyes all at once, so I told him, 'Before you tell me you love me, make sure you know everything about me!' Now he's totally freakin out...and I'm getting nervous because he looks like he's gonna beat the shit out of me. I totally froze – I didn't know what to say, and from that point he kept questioning me and saying, 'Please tell me you're joking, you can't be serious. I introduced you to my whole family, I had sex with you, and you're basically telling me you're really a MAN.' At that moment I was no longer the girl he fell in love with, I was a freak to him. He totally snapped, pulled out his gun from his closet, pointed it at my head and told me he could just shoot and kill me now. I WAS TERRIFIED! My survival tactics kicked in, and out of nowhere I just said, 'Are you fucking kidding me? I'm joking. Oh my God, you're so fucking dumb. Do me a favor and take me home now. I can't believe you just pulled a gun on me and threatened my life!' I laughed it off and played with him. Because I'm a great actress, he was totally confused and didn't know if I was joking or serious anymore, but I told him the reason why I did that was to see how he would react if we had a child, and I told him I did not approve of someone being like that and I didn't want to be with him long-term. I ended our relationship and broke up with him after that situation.

The fact of the matter is it's best to be truthful about your T and being trans. To live your life with a lie or a big secret is very hard. Someone will always clock your T or know who you are unless you move to a faraway place where no one knows you at all. I have had many girlfriends who have pussy stunted before and ended up very hurt in hospital with broken noses, jaws and ribs; and I know girls who have even ended up murdered. So please don't pussy stunt, it's not worth your life!

Sincerely,

Nikki Exotika

Pêche Di

....

Pêche Di is a model and the founder of Trans Models in New York, one of the world's first trans modelling agencies. She is also the founder of Teadate, a trans dating app. She has been featured in *The New York Times*, *Vogue* and *Cosmopolitan* and was named in the in the art and style category of the Forbes '30 Under 30' in 2017. Pêche appeared on the iconic 2014 all-trans cover of *Candy* magazine alongside trans 'royalty' such as Laverne Cox, Janet Mock and Carmen Carrera, and was also featured in Bruce Weber's all-trans Barney's campaign.

....

To my trans sisters,

Some transgender girls and boys think they're not attractive because they don't look like the people that get worshipped on social media, and that's unfortunate.

We're beautiful!

Pêche Di

Esben Esther
Pirelli Benestad

....

Esben Esther Pirelli Benestad is a Norwegian physician and sexologist who has authored numerous books and speaks internationally on sexology. She is considered one of Norway's most prominent trans people, appearing on national TV for the first time in 1994 on the popular talk show *Slightly Red*, becoming 'The National Trans of Norway'. In 2002 Esben Esther's son directed the biographical documentary film *All About My Father*, which was awarded Movie of the Year in Norway in 2002, leading to Esben Esther becoming even more well known. In 2007 she took part in the Norwegian version of the popular TV show *Dancing with the Stars*.

....

To my trans sisters,

My name is Esben Esther Pirelli Benestad. My friends call me Esben Esther. Esben is a Norwegian male name, Esther a female one. The combination is a political statement. The tire-brand name Pirelli has a long story that is actually best told in Norwegian. Benestad is the family name of my ancestors on my father's side.

It is my affirmed experience through private and professional meetings with many hundred transgifted individuals, that the talents of trans can be administrated in numerous ways and nuances.

You may meet people who seem to believe that their way is the only way, and you may meet those who do not see being trans as a talent at all, and even less as a gift – in the lives of more than one percent of the population – according to recent surveys. There are individuals who see trans, or transsexualism, as a disease that can be cured through hormones and surgeries, and there are others who do not want any bodily adjustments at all. Many are ashamed, many long for normality, many are out and proud. You may meet those who call themselves women and men, those who present as transgendered, gender queer, gender fluid, genderless, bigendered, and many other names of self-perceptions. They must choose their views, understandings and attitudes; you must choose yours. I shall not advise you in any particular direction, just render you some options of choice, and point out two major ways of finding the path you choose to walk:

You can listen to what your inner voices say, listen to your most basic wishes and needs. Those voices are closer to your particular equipment of gender(s) than those of the other way: the voices of cultures, societies, psychiatries, families, networks and fellow gender-incongruent people. The latter term is the newest and may be the most accurate. It is by any means the term that is presently most suited as an umbrella term for all of us.

Who am I to talk so knowingly of this?

For 68 years, I have walked the globe, walked with and talked to peoples of the earth, peoples of many, many cultures, societies, networks; and not least have I had numerous encounters with many, many gender incongruent individuals. I am myself transgifted (my preferred description of self), and in retrospect that talent and, by and by, that gift, have been a major part of my equipment, experienced since I was four years of age. Well, yes, you might say that the talent has always been there, and you are probably right. I can but say that I have known it since that age. I have not loved it for quite that long.

For years I was ashamed to wish for, and need to go in, this feminine direction. I was clever at being a boy. I grew into a good-looking guy, and I acquired skills in many bodily activities such as diving, waterskiing, snowskiing, swimming, climbing – you name it. Soccer, however, was not to my liking. I was not in favour of rough and tumble play. Activities linked to aesthetics were my sports of choice. I am equipped with talents to be attracted to women, and I had talents to attract women, although I was always somewhat shy, knowing that I hid a secret. I was ashamed for what I loved to do, for that which gave me so much pleasure, ashamed to want to be like a girl, ashamed to borrow my sister's and my mother's clothes, and ashamed that ever so often, when I was alone at home and had planned to spend the evening as a girl, I was overwhelmed by horniness and masturbated until all energy was drained away, and I folded every garment and put them back in closets and drawers.

By and by, shame left me. My good parents and a beautiful nanny had taught me that I was okay, even though they had no clue as to my hidden talents. In my mid-twenties, I realised that there was nothing wrong with me, but much at fault with those who were given the power to describe me as someone suffering from a gender identity disturbance. Over the decades to come, I grew increasingly convinced that I am not disturbed and as convinced that I do disturb. I realised that psychiatry, which has been convicting us to a life as mentally disturbed, had few clues about how to meet and assist talents like mine – and yours.

I became a therapist myself. First, after very good grades at the Norwegian 'Gymnasium', I studied at the University of Oslo to become a medical doctor, like my father. Thereafter, I was trained to be a family therapist, by and by a specialist in clinical sexology, and over the last 6–7 years also a full professor of that subject. I have the ambition to render the unusual human being a clean bill of health and teach societies that the uncommon human being is the one who can see the world from perspectives hidden to others. My feeling of self has moved from shame to pride, and I want to contribute to the same for you, whatever way you may move in the fields of gender.

I have been married twice, and in my first marriage I became the proud father of two children. The first, Elisabeth, has proved to be a woman; the second, Even, a man. My wife caught me red-handed in her clothes. I was at home feeding Elisabeth, and she came home to fetch something she had forgotten. I abstained from trans for a year-and-a-half after that incident. That became unbearable. My first wife by and by became an accepting, low-key supporter. Through my second marriage I have become the proud step-parent of my wife Elsa's son, Tomas. Together Elsa and I have five grandchildren. Both they and their friends call me 'Besther', and all say that 'Besther is trans.' To me this is a stigma of honour. I am a very well-known, transgifted individual in Norway, not least after my son Even's successful movie, *All About My Father*. I have been part of numerous TV programs, weekly magazine articles, newspaper interviews and comments. I have been part of Norway's version of *Dancing with the Stars* and several other entertainment programs. All openness came about on the basis of the insight that secrets do not change the world. I am the author and part-author of many books, book chapters and scientific articles.

Through my professional, and I'd like to add, my spiritual life, I have learned to appreciate the vast and beautiful complexity of nature. In this complexity, the unusual is just as self-evident as that which is common. We all arrive on the globe equipped with talents. If those talents are welcomed by our inner emotions and considerations, and also by those of our networks, they will grow into gifts. Some gifts have the power to change societies, some to change our immediate surroundings. Pride is one major mediator of all those changes. I want to enhance pride by assisting people in seeing their inner beauty.

Do not believe in those who label you sick, sinful and/or non-existent! Please, believe in that which makes you happy, in that which feels right for you, regardless of views from the outside!

That makes you beautiful.

Of course, I see that our inner views of self are highly influenced be those around us. Nevertheless, I see, and I have personally experienced, it optional to live without any template, and I think it beneficial, to the extent that we can see ourselves as shareholders in our very own company of self, that we are in possession of 51 percent of the shares. If you need to have your body adjusted, I think this is best done on your own terms, rather than on the terms of others.

For me 'passing' is cool but not at all necessary. The sorrowful thing about the need to 'pass' is the fear of not doing so. In addition, I have met individuals that 'pass' so well that they lose their narratives. They simply have no heart to tell their friends the often very interesting and challenging story of their life. The more necessary one experiences 'passing', the more it may become a straightjacket, and the more it may contribute to the shift from one closet to the other.

They have taught us not to enjoy what they have named 'autogynephilia', but they were never able to prove that autogynephilia makes anybody less woman, less trans, less anything. It just demonstrates the talent of being turned on by that which is female, womanly or just eroticized, as is much of the female wardrobe.

I once wrote:

> *There is something they call disease –*
> *Dis-ease*
> *Then, what is ease?*
> *There is something they call disorder –*
> *Dis-order*
> *Then what is order?*
> *And who decides?*

I myself enjoy my sexuality. I enjoy the merging of Elsa's and my body, including her vagina around my penis. It is not genitals that decide our gender talents, and pleasure has no gender.

I see the gender-incongruent journey as a train-ride where many seem to be heading for the same end-station, without all realizing that none of us will ever get there. We will not menstruate, we will not get pregnant, and we will never have been brought up as regular girls. Unlike the regulars, gender is something we have wished for, longed for and hopefully settled within, be our end-point prior known or unknown. Our narratives are different, and we can choose to deny or to cherish them at our own will.

We will not reach the pre-defined end-station in full, but there are certainly many possible end-points to our gender-paths, and each end-point is as valuable as the other, as long as it renders peace of mind and body, and also renders welcoming relationships to those of your chosen networks.

Your full transition is from where you start to where you find your end-station, be it one that is more or less known or one that is not yet described.

I venture to advise you to stop regularly at stations, as you move forward on your journey. Stay there long enough to find out if you have reached far enough, or if you are to board the train to travel on to the next stop.

Take care of your sexuality, whichever way that may take you, as long as you harass no one. There is no such thing as the right way to administrate the turn-on talents of trans-talented individuals; there is no such thing as a right way to have sex or to be horny. The best way for you is simply your way and at best, also that of your partner(s).

I have, through hormones, minor surgery and laser hair-removal treatment, adjusted my body according to my wishes and needs and not in major opposition to my spouse. She is the love of my life, my companion in private and professional life. I do not live *in vacuo*, I always find myself in relations to Elsa, my children, grandchildren, clients, friends and fellow human beings. No one has to my knowledge rejected me. My father had reached an advanced age when he first met me as a woman, and thereafter he became an active supporter. Both he and my mother had pride in my trans talents. My children were informed of my talents when they were about 11–12 years of age. Today, they say this was way too late. They felt there was secrecy in their childhood, but never understood the background. That was uncomfortable for them. Elsa and I have numerous friends both in Norway and elsewhere. Many of them will not be able to remember whether at any meeting we have had, I expressed myself as a male or a female. I consider myself as neither. My gender is trans, and that gender has no demands outside my own wishes and needs.

I want to share with you a poem I wrote some years ago. It came into being as I met with the Volcano Goddess, Pele, of Hawaii.

With love and hugs and a train load of pride:

Pele

This tale I tell about to be,
was handed forcefully to me
by land and sea of Hawaii.

Once – very deep on ocean floor
some furious force flung out a door,
and from this spot of heated rock
came one by one an island flock.
A holy act of giving birth,
was thus performed by Mother Earth.

That row of islands clad in green,
- for nameless times the sun has seen,
- as they most slowly moved up north,
- that coat of green was coming forth.

Sun's rays of power day by day,
did foster wonders from the clay.
As all around the hands of sea
gave seeds for all the fruits to be.

We came by air, on manmade wings,
to hear and watch the ways of things.
I bore a restlessness in me.
A restlessness one names: To be.

I house my being bodily,
as bodily I hear and see.
My soul, however, won't agree

my body to be fully me
- though:
We cannot leave our body shell,
although it may not suit us well.
Like all the islands in the row,
must stick to Mother Earth somehow.

I had two fruitful nights of rest,
and felt quite close to very best,
then once again I went by plane
to reach Volcano's own domain.

I watched her form from way up high,
as sea and land below went by.
Her surface wrinkled, grey and broken,
secluded secrets not yet spoken.

I spent a day of distant mind,
some quaking quest left all behind.
The night that came gave meagre sleep,
the restlessness derived from deep.

Some force disturbed behind my back,
I could not rest, I lost my track.
Thus time went by in painful waves,-
That is how restlessness behaves.
I was so stubbornly awake,
I prayed for rest – for Heaven's sake.

I closed my eyes and counted sheep.
The sleep that came was calm and deep.
I left the empty feel of tomb,
and made an entry to a womb.

In that secluded cavity,
I lost my sense of gravity.

I heard a voice from way behind,
it took me in, it caught my mind.
It was so forceful, calm and sweet.
Who-ever spoke – we had to meet.

And there she came in steady pace,
her arms wide opened for embrace.
She caught my glance, and held me tight.
She said:
'Let's render you good rest tonight.
I see your pain, your dark turmoil.
I know it by my link to soil.

I hand you clarity if you desire.
I am the deity of heat and fire.'

I smiled and said: 'I must confess:
I ask no more, I pray no less!'

'Then talk to me', she said, 'and tell!
We need to know to make you well.
Whatever trembles in your mind,
it must by tale be left behind.'

She led me by her friendly hand
on to her cracked and wrinkled land.
We slowly walked her glow-paved street,
I felt a warmth rise through my feet –
a warmth unsteady, incomplete.
She softly spoke: 'We are in heat!'

'I know,' I said, 'I've known for years,
and shed from heat a sea of tears,
and seen my inner, sacred stage
be battleground for wrath and rage,
but from this rage so long compressed,
I have but minor wrath expressed!

'My path was stony – in distress.
What was this hell, this painful mess?'
'I have', she said, 'one only guess:
You sensed the well of loneliness!'

'It takes,' I said, 'that I can tell,
a lot to face that deep, dark well!'

She answered smilingly: 'To cope –
just see it as kaleidoscope.

A fertile, twinkling treasure bin,
your deep and sacred womb within.
I tell you here and now, to night:
It can but be conceived by light.'

'And then,' I asked, 'how shall I act,
when light has rendered its impact?'

'Then day by day you have to rise
and face the scrutiny of eyes.
There is a troubled lot to do,
before they see the same as you.
You must reveal, you must declare
to gain a sense of being here.

'From every pit, each glowing hole,
through manly spirits I control.
I must, myself, burst out in fire.
My yearn for being does require
that I express my gleaming heat.
Secluded powers spell defeat.
By fire's aid, I rise up high,
from heat alone, I fade and die.

'You must give birth to be alive,
from whatever source your births derive.
Birth is by any way of seeing,
the ground for all array of being!

'From heat grows rage, from wrath rises fire,
you choose your ways as you desire.
But will you take a kind advice,
you choose the warmth and melt the ice.
Lead rage to heat, leave wrath for fire,
and you shall meet what you admire.'

I sensed through trembling well so steep
the shift of magma in my deep.
It was alive my very soul,
I heaved in yearning to be whole.
I could erupt at any time –
in hot cascades or more sublime.

I saw myself in smoke and flame
give rise to wild, to fierce to tame.
I felt as ripe as budding spring
and ready for most anything.

Though-
before eruption came to be,
The Goddess, Pele, spoke to me:

'*We have encountered sweet as brothers,*
like we did meet as heated mothers.
We have both sensed the inner urge,
to let our powers meet and merge.
It takes a motherhood of soul
to merge such forces to a whole.
It takes some qualities of male,
to let erupt such forceful tale.

'*As we inhale, as we expire,*
we must for light and tale inquire.
We own a well of some extremes,
that can make living Hell it seems.

'*To seat a wholesome rest require:*
To mother heat and father fire.'

Hawaii, Maui, Oahu, February 13–22, 2000

Sincerely,

Esben Esther

Justine Smithies

....

Justine Smithies is best known for starring in the BBC documentary *Transgender Love*, where she and her wife shared their incredible relationship with the world. She is a marine electronics engineer and does a lot of trans advocacy work, speaking all over the UK about trans inclusion in education and the workplace. Justine is also a patron of the charity LGBT History Project NE.

....

To my trans sisters,

I'm really glad that you're reading this letter, I hope I can pass on a little advice that I really wish someone had shared with me before I came out and transitioned.

Firstly, I probably say this too much, but I cannot stress enough that you must live your life by your rules and nobody else's. As you're only on this planet once, please just be yourself.

If you're worrying about telling your friends or family, please don't. You'll be surprised by the supportive reactions that you'll get, but there will be some people that you probably thought would support you throughout this that don't. Don't let them put you off becoming your authentic self; life is so much better when you can just be you. As I said, there might be those that reject you, but to be honest how can they be real family or friends if they cannot help you through this journey? Trust me, you will make loads of new friends and some you'll come to think of as family too.

When you go out shopping for clothes, take my advice and ignore what is going on around you. I spent far too much time watching others who I thought had clocked me just because they happened to look at me and were laughing with others. Believe me when I say this – it was my own paranoia making me think that everyone I saw looking or laughing even cared who I was. In reality they were laughing with their friends and hadn't even noticed me at all. Our minds play some horrible tricks on us, making us think that everything going on around us is about us when in reality it is not!

I'm going to try and talk about some of the things that you really need to get sorted and some things that nobody told me until it was too late. Please don't self-medicate by purchasing hormones off the Internet as I did to start with! You really don't know what is actually in them and they could do you more harm than good. Also by doing it yourself you'll not get proper access to the blood tests that you'll require to check that everything is going according to plan with regards to hormone levels and liver function tests etc. Go and see your doctor and don't be afraid, they might not be knowledgeable on the topic, many aren't, mine wasn't – but he went away and did his research so that he could help me. Hey, if neither of you know the answers, use the web or find an online support group. You'll find loads of people in the same situation willing to help and those like myself that have been there, done that and got the t-shirt. Yes, you'll have to talk about stuff that you'd rather not talk about, but please don't be frightened as there are no stupid questions or answers. You'll also want to find out about hair removal, be it electrolysis or laser. I was lucky as I wasn't really that hairy. I just had some facial hair but no body hair so laser worked just fine for me. But what I wasn't told until I got my gender reassignment surgery (GRS) referral was that I should have had my downstairs lasered too! This set my GRS back a whole year, so please, please do get this sorted too! You might get it done by a National Health Service (NHS) clinic or you may, like myself, have to go private – I chose to go to a SK:N clinic. Don't worry, you'll not be the first or the last trans person that they have had come through their doors. I can't tell you what electrolysis feels like, but laser to me feels like someone flicking an elastic band at you very quickly, over and over. It's not agony, but it does make your face a tad red and toasty afterwards, but it's well worth it for the end effect.

Changing your name is a piece of cake and you can do this with either a deed poll or a statutory declaration, depending on where you are. You can do these online or go through a solicitor. Once that is done, just send copies to absolutely every company you have dealings with to inform them of your name change – and, yes, you can change your title too, so don't let anyone tell you any different. Oh, and don't forget the electoral register! If you're old enough, you can change your gender, title and name on your driving licence too by getting a form from the Driver and Vehicle Licensing Agency (DVLA). If you are in work, telling your employer can be very intimidating. I know I was terrified and ready to be told to collect my things and go, so I was very surprised to be offered all the help that they could give me; they were extremely supportive. Just remember that they cannot fire you just because you are trans, and the law is on your side.

I work as a marine electronics engineer based in Peterhead. My job involves installing and repairing satellite internet and television, radars, radio and autopilots on everything from yachts and fishing vessels to oil-supply ships and rigs. I live in a very religious community; women do not work on the fishing boats and nobody ever talked about trans folk or even being gay, so me coming out was a complete shock to everyone and some of the fishermen found it difficult at first. I was told not to work on their boats, and they would just walk off whilst I worked; but in time, after seeing that I wasn't going to run away and would answer their questions and educate them, the whole community began to accept me. In fact, I have made more friends than I have ever had in my life.

I've gone from someone who wouldn't even have the courage to go for a coffee on my own in a strange city to someone who now gives talks at educational establishments and businesses on transgender inclusivity and at various prides around the UK. So you can see that I'm living proof that it can be OK and that being transgender does not stop you from achieving anything that you want in life.

I really hope that something I've said in this letter has helped or given you the strength to become your true self – and you never know, one day our paths may cross! Until then, know that you are valid and that you are loved!

Hugs and kisses,

Justine Smithies

Vanessa Lopez

....

Vanessa Lopez is a former model and media personality who was the first openly transgender person in Scandinavia to participate in a reality show, starring on the popular TV show *Big Brother Sweden* in 2011. After leaving the house, she authored a memoir, *Jag har ångrat mig* (*I've changed my mind*), and went on to win the Miss Trans Star International contest in 2015, representing her native country, Chile.

....

To my trans sisters,

If you are planning on undergoing reassignment surgery, I want you to think about this: Do you think that gender dysphoria would exist in an individual, if transphobia didn't exist? Do you think that it is you who is born in the wrong body or are you only born under the wrong norms and society?

Being transgender can be challenging in so many ways, but remember that we are an important part of humanity. We are the ones that question the status quo and the gender norms, which are the norms that have most influence on people. We are here to serve our fellow humans, to liberate them from the chains of the binary system. Gender and sexuality are fluid and can change through life.

When I started my transition at the age of 16 I wish that I'd had a coach who empowered me and taught me that there was never anything wrong with my body; that somebody had taught me humans are not born with self-hate – not even transgender people. Why do we really feel we need so much surgery?

It took so many years for me to see the positive aspects of being transgender. Our perspective used to be celebrated in many cultures across the world. We were considered super humans because we were blessed with being both male and female in the same body. And that is how I define myself today: as a woman and a man at the same time. Don't hate your male features, embrace them. It is beautiful to have the characteristics of both man and woman in the same body. It hurts so much to see transgender people hating their ambiguity. If only we were accepted and loved by society, then we wouldn't want to change our bodies as much as we do.

Today we want to pass as either women or men, so we can be happy with ourselves, so we can feel loved, appreciated and respected.

So before you make any big decisions about major surgery, think about this: If we never experienced transphobia, would we ever hate our bodies? Would we ever want to do major surgeries to change a perfectly functioning body part?

I think it is tragic that we have to be the ones that have to change ourselves to be able to feel accepted by society, but I understand that it helps some transgender people to accept themselves and to live a dignified day-to-day life.

At the end of the day, I'm very happy with my sex reassignment surgery (SRS). It has helped prevent me from developing male characteristics and it has helped me to stay feminine, which has helped me to survive my day-to-day life, free from prejudice. So do what you have to do to survive in our society, because it will take at least a generation before transgender people start to be accepted by society.

In the future, being transgender will not be a big deal. In the future, we trans people will embrace our ambiguity and we will redefine what it is to be transgender and how we deal with our bodies.

Vanessa Lopez

Lana Lawless

....

Lana Lawless made history in 2007 as the first transgender woman to compete as a professional female golfer in the Remax World Long Drive Championship, finishing in third place. She then returned a year later, finishing first. In 2010, after being banned from competing as a professional female golfer by the World Long Drive Association (WLDA) and the Ladies Professional Golf Association (LPGA), she took legal action against these organisations, forcing both of them to remove their bans stopping transgender individuals from competing. Prior to her professional golfing career and transition, she worked in the police department in the Special Weapons and Tactics (SWAT) and gang unit for 20 years.

....

To my trans sisters,

Here are a few hopefully helpful hints from Auntie Lana:

Passing in public – we all want to live our lives without any added drama and, yeah, dressing like a hooker at high noon to go to the mall or market (unless you are one...then great) doesn't help; but, hey, if that's your style then rock it... Just remember that in life, for every action there is a reaction... Could be positive, could be negative. Only time will tell.

After I told a friend (who was trans and already living 24/7 as a female) that I was going to fully transition, she said, 'That's great sweetie, but remember you're about to get on a horse that never stops bucking.' She wasn't lying, but that's part of the gig. This life, this journey isn't for the faint of heart, but no one ever said the journey would be easy; just worth it.

Me, I might look like Vanna White, but I sound like Barry White. I turned that around and made it work for me! My friend also told me back then when going out in public – to the mall, market or anywhere during the day in public view – was terrifying, 'Sweetie, the day will come when you no longer think, "Are people looking at me? Am I passing?" And when that day comes...welcome, you've made it; you are who you were meant to be..."LANA". At that point girl-world is no longer about fetish or fantasy... Girl-world for me and my sisters at that point, well, it's just another day.'

Think about it, all passing really is...a convenience, that's all. We are who we are, inside and out... I look OK and pass a lot (either that or people are just nice to me, and that's fine too), but I have days when it's a being clocked festival... It's called 'life'.

You have to want this, this life; face all the negative crap the world has to give, lose family, friends, maybe your job and all the hatred...and stand tall. When I'm asked 'Why would you do that?' my answer is only three words... 'Because Lana lives'... That makes it all worth it.

If you want it bad enough, you have to fight for it, facing all the negative along with all the good and awesomeness of being your true self.

Food for thought: in the police academy they taught us 'the will to survive', which means if someone punches you in the mouth and knocks out your teeth, you swallow them and keep fighting... So take that mental attitude to all walks of life... The point is, you NEVER QUIT!!

Hope this helps,

Lana

Christina Riley

....

Christina Riley is senior planning manager at Balfour Beatty, a British multinational construction and infrastructure group. She is said to be one of the first trans women to come out in the construction industry, and her role sees her working on some of the largest projects in the UK. She is Chair of the Balfour Beatty LGBT Network. In both 2015 and 2016 Christina was named in the OUTstanding Future Leaders Awards, published in the *Financial Times*, and won a British LGBT Award in the Corporate Rising Star category in 2017. Christina speaks across the country at conferences on LGBT inclusion in business, and at schools through the Diversity Role Models programme. She was featured on the *Independent on Sunday*'s Rainbow List as 'one to watch'.

....

To my trans sisters,

Wow, congratulations, you've just made the best decision of your life in reading this book.

Why?

Because you know who you really are, and are looking for support to help you make some sense of this all.

You picked up this book, perhaps confused about your gender identity, or perhaps you already know your gender identity but just don't know how to express it to the big wide world. Let me tell you this: I was where you are once, not too long ago. But I found myself...and I found many others like me who are today successful in life.

They too found confidence and true authenticity.

My letter begins with where I am today.

So you are transgender. You may be gender fluid. You may be non-binary.

Now, I know transgender people who are, believe it or not, just treated as people. Where being trans is irrelevant.

I know trans people who are successful in all these careers:

- airline pilot
- architect
- police officer
- army officer
- navy officer
- police helicopter pilot
- nurse
- doctor
- lawyer
- design consultant
- bus driver
- journalist
- film director
- software engineer
- railway analyst
- teacher.

And me, I'm a construction industry planning manager. I work on construction sites, coming into contact with everyone from the bricklayer to the roofer, to the painter to the kitchen fitter, to the architect to the structural engineer, on some of the largest projects in the UK.

So why am I telling you this? How is this relevant to transition?

Because you may not realise this, but the biggest barrier is your own confidence. There are plenty of positive role models out there! It's the 21st century – we still have our challenges, and society over the last few years feels like it has become more polarised, with homophobia and transphobia on the rise in some corners of the world, but you can draw strength knowing that there is support out there. You don't even have to look too far.

OK, so you say, 'Where do I look?'

Take a look at pride events.

Take a look at how many businesses attend.

So how is this relevant? Well it goes back to confidence in being yourself.

Be yourself and you will find your way through life, and you will succeed.

OK, so now I am going to go back to when I first knew I was transgender. I doubt the word even existed when I was five in 1975. Yet gender variance has been around forever, and society has grown in confidence in being able to talk about gender identity. This is why I do public speaking on LGBT inclusion in business. I also speak in schools with Diversity Role Models under LGBT Construct, and I see that homophobic and transphobic language is still very prevalent in our education system between children. Bullying can rear its ugly head – sometimes with terrible consequences – and I understand that bullying or anxiety about bullying may be what's holding you back from coming out.

My advice is to first educate yourself on support groups. Charities like Mermaids, Diversity Role Models and Stonewall are the best place to start. There are also anti-bullying charities, and charities that support your family. It's tough, but be strong in yourself.

So this brings me onto family. I was terrified of having to tell my wife and children. And how do you tell your mum or your dad?! Keeping my gender identity a secret was taking a toll and I was quite ill with chronic anxiety, suffering from panic attacks for ten years. I know for some, this has led to people taking their own life. Suicide is so common in our community. But I could never do it. Life is too precious. You may be down, you may have hard times, but one thing I was told a long time ago, was this: 'Things never stay the same. Times change, and situations change. People change.' Things always get better. I would encourage you, if you feel suicidal, to please contact the Samaritans, who will support you through your thoughts and feelings.

So with family and gender identity, how do you balance the two if you feel a bad reaction from relations? For me, I was prepared to lose my family and friends in order to find myself, to get healthy again, and to move forward with my transition.

You will have to make hard decisions. And, yes, you may lose some family, as well as perhaps some of your closest friends. So I made the hardest decision of my life, and that was to sit in my parents' lounge, and give my mum and dad a copy of my coming out letter. This is a copy of it, unchanged from the day I gave it to them:

Dear Mum, Dad...I love you...

I am writing to you because the time has come that I cannot keep something from you. It is not a bad thing but it is

281

something you will need help to understand. I love you for all your guidance in my life. The values you both taught me will be with me forever...

A small minority of people who know about this already have bad intentions in trying to expose my issues ahead of when I am ready. And so I can't keep this quiet any more.

For many years I was quite ill with extreme panic attacks. Chronic anxiety and occasional depression. Symptoms were frightening and I suffered daily palpitations and disabling panic attacks both in the day-time and asleep. At work, on the train, at home, everywhere.

The chronic anxiety lasted over 10 years and I was on a mixture of betablockers and antidepressants including valium. At the time I struggled and became quite withdrawn, analysing my symptoms and worrying constantly. I was not greatly supported in the marriage...

In around 2005 I had the most frightening panic attack I have ever had. A huge thump in the chest (bigger and worse than any of the others and blood being drawn from the extremes of my body... I felt I was almost certainly going to die).

It was on this day that I knew I had to see my doctor and tell him why I had such disabling chronic anxiety and I needed major medical help. The panic attacks were almost hourly, and daily, and getting worse.

The only way I could get better was to go through acceptance of why I was ill... The reason was for years I knew I was transgendered and was suppressing my true inner feelings, emotions, personal embarrassment, stresses, etc.

So, what is transgender?

It is when a person of one gender (male) feels their true gender is the opposite sex (female).

I can't hide this anymore as it has made me very ill for so long, so I hope you can understand that for me coming to terms with myself has taken many years and self acceptance has helped me recover from years of illness. To a point now where the anxiety has completely gone. I no longer need the years of medication that helped control the anxiety.

I have had a lot of counselling and medical help to come to terms with this over the last 7 years and it has helped me no end.

I am happier than I have been for years and I have more friends and support than I have had for years. For years I have not invited you around the flat or house because I dress in female clothing in the daytime. I have lost valuable time in having a closer bond with you and friends and family.

How do I live my life? Well I have many clothes. I have many friends in the community and in a normal capacity that only know me in female mode. Socially more people talk to me and support me. I go out in the daytime to many different places, whether to London, Bristol, Cardiff, Manchester. Shopping, driving, and even filling up with petrol. Last week I went to an air show with 100,000 people without any worries.

I have true friends now. Better friends and real friends. Even colleagues at work know including the management and their support has been amazing beyond words.

To a point where I am now on two committees looking at recruitment and diversity in the company and mixing with directors on the issue. It has opened more doors for me than I could ever imagine.

In terms of image, I am just a smart, beautiful person, and I am so proud of myself and where I have come from. I always tell people I hope one day my parents can see the whole me. They would be proud.

Lastly, the children. Charlotte and Rebecca don't yet know, but they will soon. It is now impossible to hide. I have a support system in place to help them understand this. There are lots of organisations that support families that go through this.

My best friend is transgender. Kirsty. She has two children and they are the happiest children I have ever seen. It can work if done carefully, sensitively and with a support network that is structured and there for them when they need it.

I am still Chris. It is just a renewed happy Chris. With a good network of support that has been there for a long time. I am sure about myself. This has been with me for 20 years or more and I have finally found the person I am meant to be. I love you both and I know you will struggle with this, but I want you to be proud of me, and see this is a better me...

For the first time in my life I am doing the things I love. The band is amazing. I do my Star Wars conventions and river kayaking. And then I can be my female self. A lot of people only know me as the female Chris and that makes me proud that I am accepted totally.

I hope in your hearts you can see this hasn't been an easy journey for me, and I don't pretend it will be easy for you to come to terms with. But our family is built on love. It is built on good morals. On respect and kindness. Values that I have given my children.

One of the greatest values we learned from you both as parents is understanding and compassion for people who suffer. I have suffered. But now I am in the best place I have ever been. Happier than I have ever been.

I hope you can see that this doesn't change me. I am still me. Still the same person I was yesterday. The same person today... Like a book, I just have another cover, a beautiful cover, but the story inside is the same.

Mum, Dad... I will love you always. Thank you for always being there for me...

So I told them, and the silence was the longest I have experienced in my life. Their reaction was one of surprise and shock. My Dad struggled, I can tell you, and those first eight weeks felt strained afterwards. That was October 2014...but in December that year I spent Christmas Day as Christina with my Mum and Dad, and we had a wonderful time. In a short time, our family had come a long way to support me, and both parents fully support me then and today. But I also struggled with my teenage children. A counsellor told them about my transition, and it has taken around two years for them to be quite relaxed that they have a transgender dad. We now go out as a family without even a thought.

For them, I have tried to lead by example, by being involved in many LGBT events and organisations, and speaking publicly about my journey to help others. This, I hope, has given them inspiration to be proud of me as their dad, and for them to be confident in themselves about having a transgender parent.

So, lastly, the actual transition process – start as soon as you feel you can, because full medical transition can take five to six years through the National Health Service (NHS). However, I have now lived full-time in my authentic gender for nearly three years. I feel I have made it. Final surgery will be in 2018, but for me, a few more months won't stop me being authentic. It will just be the last piece of the jigsaw of transition. But it's not the end of my journey, as it will give me new opportunities, particularly with social interaction. For the first time I will be able to wear clothes that match my gender, for example, in sports like swimming.

Other aspects of transitioning – it will take at least four years through the NHS, or you can go private. Start living full time asap so that you can start hormone treatment. Start your laser treatment as soon as you can. I can tell you laser is not permanent. You may want to try electrolysis, but I found my skin became quite bruised, so I had to take a break from the treatment. Voice coaching is provided on the NHS, but it is hard work and lots of practice is recommended, but the NHS can provide a number of sessions to help you.

So this brings me back to today. I am writing this to you sat on a train, travelling for my work from Exeter to Oxford. If I told myself I would be doing this four years ago I would have said it was impossible, that it could never happen. I don't know how it could happen. Being on a packed commuter train or on an underground train is the ultimate in terms of invasion of your personal space, with everyone breathing down each other's neck. But I can say I do this every week. It's not an issue. I just turn up and get on the train. I walk on to building sites and just do my job. But today I do it as Christina.

So back to the start, if I can do it, you can too, and you will.

Take care, sis, take your time, be strong, and above all be confident and you will find yourself.

Christina

Baby Dee

....

Baby Dee is a musician and songwriter. She began her career on the streets of New York as a winged cat on a high-rise, concert harp-laden tricycle, playing accordion to great acclaim. Her songwriting took a serious turn in 1999 and since then she has gone on to release several albums and to tour extensively throughout Europe and North America. Her songs have been embraced and sung by Academy Award-nominated Anohni, Marc Almond and many others.

....

To my trans sisters,

I would think, or at least hope, that for a transgender kid young enough to be my grandchild, allowing oneself to be oneself is, or at least ought to be, self-evident – of course you must allow yourself to be yourself!

What am I saying? I'm saying it ought to be unthinkable to live your life as a lie. It ought to be unthinkable for someone to have to keep their head down in some sort of 'safe place' of the wrong kind of self-denial – in hiding from one's inconveniently true self.

And yet, I did just that. And I can tell anybody, straight up, that it's not a good idea. And the longer you put it off, the greater the harm. So, yes, be who you are and fight your corner. And for God's sake don't wait until you're in your late thirties to experience adolescence – it's way too embarrassing!

So anyway, I wish you love – tons of love from every which way. And luck – that you fall in with wonderful friends. And money – because you're probably going to need some of that too. (Not billions though. We're up to our eyeballs in billionaires these days and they seem to be running things. I mean, ask yourself, what kind an asshole wants to be a billionaire? And they think we've got problems!)

Don't get discouraged. When you reach the limit of what you can endure in terms of plain human meanness, then let yourself rage. But in your rage say this: 'Life – my life (and here you poke yourself in the chest like an orangutan or a beer boy) – is going to get better!'

And it will. I promise you it will.

Love,

Baby Dee

Naomi Fontanos

....

Naomi Fontanos is a Filipina activist. She is one of the founders and current Executive Director of transgender rights group Gender and Development Advocates (GANDA) Filipinas, whose aim is to locate trans activism in the framework of human rights. In 2011, Naomi, along with two other Filipina trans women, petitioned the United Nations Human Rights Committee, asking them to compel the government of the Philippines to address the situation facing transgender Filipinos. Naomi is also a writer and public speaker on trans issues.

....

To my trans sisters,

As you read this, imagine that I am holding both of your hands and you can feel the glowing warmth of my touch in your heart. Imagine too that I am right there in front of you, reassuring you that you are on the right track and we are basking in the shimmer of our sisterhood.

My dearest sisters, how wonderful that you have decided to start your transition! That you have reached this point and been able to make this choice to embrace who you truly are is indeed a gift. In fact, mine I considered a gift of life.

In the Philippines, many women like us like to say that we really do not transition. Instead, we blossom. Because many of us are already very feminine at a young age, becoming the woman outside that we feel we are inside is really just a matter of time. I had my first taste of feminizing hormones when I was 19 years old and in college. But my struggle with my gender identity started as early as five years old.

I was five years old when I had the first inkling that I was supposed to be a girl. Prior to that, there were signs. After taking a bath one time, I stood in front of the mirror with my genitals tucked between my thighs, and thought that this was what my body should look like. Another time, I placed a towel over my head like a wig and imagined myself with very long hair. I have never felt so beautiful. Then another time, I saw a new dress made for my older sister for her birthday and I couldn't resist putting it on. I did and jumped in front of my mother to surprise her, thinking how happy she'd be. She was not. She got very angry and upset and ordered me to take the dress off. That was the first time I learned that in order to stay out of trouble and to keep the peace and not upset the people around me including my immediate family, I had to hide who I was and bury that person deep inside.

So I played the part of a dutiful 'son' and finished high school at the top of my class. When I entered the Philippines' top university, the University of the Philippines Diliman, my gender struggles resurfaced. It was as if everything that I had kept hidden could no longer be contained inside. I fell into a deep sadness upon realizing that if I didn't become the girl I always thought I was, I would be worse than dead. I had to accept who I was meant to be and become the woman that I was inside if I wanted to live. So I did.

Many of us cover up who we are for so long that when we finally decide to link fingers with the person we were always meant to be, it feels like an erosion of the many years of sadness and regret. It's like clambering out of a deep, dark hole of miserable self-hatred into the liberating light of joyful self-acceptance. Sisters, you are not alone in this journey. There are women like us who came before you, and there will be women like us who will come after you.

Our connection will be this gift of transition, of becoming, of blossoming into the brave, bold and beautiful human beings that we are. Hold on tight. Through this letter, I am holding your hand as you bloom. May your own radiance shine ever brightly that it would take another sister by the hand into the light.

With love,

Naomi Fontanos

Kate O'Donnell

....

Kate O'Donnell is an award-winning transgender performer, activist and the Artistic Director of Trans Creative. Her previous work includes the award-winning autobiographical *Big Girl's Blouse*, *Hayley and Me*, *A Short History of My Tits* and *No Pride*. Most recently she appeared as the first trans woman to play the role of Feste in Jo Davies' *Twelfth Night* at the Royal Exchange in Manchester, and starred in the BBC's groundbreaking *Boy Meets Girl*. An advocate for trans rights, she has spoken at the Women of the World Festival, and in 2015 was awarded the LGBT foundation's Hero Award.

....

To my trans sisters,

If being transgender was a job, no one would apply for it. I am not sure how the job description would read, or what the pay would be like, but take it from me, you will not be rich. It costs a lot to transition. Think electrolysis, prescriptions, deed poll name changes, gender recognition certificates, a new wardrobe and then there is always surgery. I funded most of this by remortgaging my house. I said it was for home improvements!

How about the working conditions? Well, it's a mixture of awkward and embarrassing moments: you may be challenged about which toilet you can use or be called the wrong gender on a daily basis. You may be threatened verbally or physically and regularly have to field questions about what's between your legs.

The big perk of the job is, even though it's scary and hard, you get to be you. More of us are finding the strength to transition and take on the job of being transgender. The level of admin required means it really is a job – just think about changing every document your name appears on.

Some people are too frightened to transition and I understand why. How the job is advertised in the press, media, TV and film is hardly positive. I applied for the job 14 years ago. Back then it was all about living in stealth. Trans people, myself included, hid themselves. There were no fabulous trans pride events like there are today. My ex boyfriend's family never knew I was trans (at my boyfriend's request). They still don't officially know. Concealing my past involved lots of awkward conversations about the fact I had not had children and having to reinvent bits of my past. That's what I hated the most: having to make up a cisgendered past. My queer, gay male, drag queen, trans past was so much more interesting!

The job has become a lot more exciting for me in the last three years since I truly outed myself and stepped into the spotlight, starting to make theatre work about being trans. I did this because I didn't see my story represented on stage. And let's face it, I am also a big show-off. Basically, I rewrote my own job description, creating an uplifting piece of theatre which made a song and dance about being trans. The show is called *Big Girl's Blouse*, a name my dad called me on a daily basis, just as his way of letting me know what a shit dad he was.

I toured the show for two years up and down the country, did Q&As after each show, created an online campaign encouraging visibility and solidarity for the transgender community and wore my accompanying t-shirt at every opportunity. I went on radio, appeared in BBC 2's *Boy Meets Girl*, hosted events, appeared in magazines, was in a gender musical, created cabaret pieces, took my clothes off, wrote songs with a trans jazz musician – basically anything to make people see trans people in a new light: a positive light. Trans people are often shown as sad, lonely people, or as sex workers, or trapped in the wrong body, rejected, suicidal, killed or simply dead. Basically, the media would have you believe that it never ends well for us trans folk.

I believe that art can create social change and I like being part of that change. Once, during the Q&A session after one of my shows a young person came out to their mum about their gender identity on stage – a live transition. As a trans person you can be very isolated. Creating and touring the *Big Girl's Blouse* show helped me meet so many amazing trans people. I now feel a part of this incredibly exciting community, and I now have a trans boyfriend to boot!

There has been a tidal wave of interest in all things trans, which has quickly increased visibility for the community. However, with visibility can come vulnerability. For me as a trans performer more doors are now open for me than ever before, which means I am now able to open some doors for others. I have just received three years' funding from the Arts Council's Elevate fund to form a trans theatre company called Trans Creative. Our mission is to be trans led, trans positive and of course, trans creative. I am rehearsing the role of Feste the fool (typecast!) in Shakespeare's gender-bending play *Twelfth Night* at The Royal Exchange in Manchester. In this production, Feste, who is traditionally cast as a man, has transitioned. Exploring the character's lines, which were written over 500 years ago, has been a very interesting experience. At the end of the show, I, as a trans woman, sing a song in which the first line is 'When that I was a little boy.' In today's rehearsals I cried whilst singing as it struck such a chord.

We have come a long way. Of course, there is still much more to do, but I believe the job of being transgender will get better as we get prouder and happier at being transgender, as more doors are open to us and we are shown in better lights. Here's to better working conditions and a few more perks of the job.

Kate O'Donnell

Aimee Challenor

....

Aimee Challenor is the Equalities (LGBTIQA+) Spokesperson for the Green Party of England and Wales, and Chair of LGBTIQ Greens. She is also a trustee of Coventry Pride and writes regularly about LGBTIQA+ issues for the *Huffington Post* on topics including LGBT asylum-seekers, trans healthcare and queer politics.

....

To my trans sisters,

You're starting an amazing journey, you are being yourself, you're being brave. You're growing up, coming out, taking control of your body. It won't be easy. There will be many challenges, from hateful bigots to doctor delays, there will be rejection, depression, bullying. But there will also be support, love, friends, success.

Be proud to be yourself, be proud of who you are.

Whether you are in school, college or work, there will be people who have got your back, people who support you. There is a massive supportive community, and we will fight for you, we will continue to change the law, we will continue to change attitudes, we will fight for our rights.

You may face a long road ahead; it may look winding and scary. It is, but it is so worth it. You are worth it. So as you face that long road, remember that we will be by your side. This is not a journey you have to make alone. Together we will make that road less winding, we will make it less scary, and we will make positive change.

Dear sis, you are awesome, and I am proud of you.

Aimee Challenor

Donna Whitbread

Donna Whitbread is best known for starring in Channel 4's groundbreaking *My Transsexual Summer*, a documentary series that followed seven trans people on their paths to realising their true identities. Since the show in 2011, she has continued to advocate for the trans community. Donna is also a professional performer, specialising in fire-eating.

To my trans sisters,

I would like to tell you a bit about dating as a transsexual woman.

Dating is stressful enough for anyone, but add being trans into the mix and that can make it seem almost impossible. As a transsexual woman, nurturing a relationship can be difficult, but not impossible. I know many trans people in successful relationships, many are even married.

Being trans doesn't mean you can only date within the transsexual community. There are trans men in hetero-sexual relationships with cis women, and trans women in heterosexual relationships with cis men. There are trans men in gay relationships and trans and cis women in lesbian relationships. The combinations go on and on. It is important not to worry where you will fit in with all of this, but to try and understand what will make you happy.

You must always remember your self-worth; never sell yourself short.

Many transsexuals feel that they must 'make do' and that any relationship is better than none. While understandable, this is not the case. To 'make do' or to settle for anything less than what makes you truly happy is in fact the opposite to everything that, as a transsexual, you have fought for, but this is a personal process of evolution.

It is easy to get stuck in a situation where, as a transsexual, you are with somebody that doesn't want to go out on dates with you and feels more comfortable staying in where nobody will see that they are in a relationship with a 'tranny'. I have been in this situation and it was soul-destroying trying to get my 'partner' to venture out, when his constant excuse was 'I am not ready'; and more telling was when he saw me in public and he blanked me.

This is not to be confused with someone who simply needs a period of adjustment. All new relationships come with an amount of uncertainty and some people simply don't want to be pigeonholed as 'taken' when they are still finding their feet, as it were. Trust your own feelings and you will know when it is just someone who is taking it slowly with a view to a long-term relationship or someone who's literally just along for the ride. None of us are freaks, none of us deserve to only be loved in the dark. We have nothing to be ashamed of!

I was once asked, if I could go back in time and give my younger self some advice, what would this advice be? It's a difficult question, there are so many things I would protect myself from, but mainly, I would say: 'When you feel down, it won't last long.

When you think you are alone, you are not. When you think there is nobody for you, it is just your mind playing tricks on you.'

I believe we are perfect the way we are, but if this is not who you think you are, then you are right to seek to change it. There are many who see your light and many who will support and guide you. Don't rush, don't settle for less. Life is for living and you will find your place. It may not be easy, but in the end you will belong. Remember, if it's not worth working for, it's not worth having. Love yourself.

I leave you with this thought – if your future self came back, what advice would you give yourself?

Donna Whitbread

Amy Tashiana

....

Amy Tashiana, known as the Diva of Singapore, is a former model and performer from Singapore, who was signed to Carrie models and known as one of the top trans models of her time. Nowadays she is a mother figure to the LGBTQ community in Singapore and runs a very popular online cooking show, *Masak Apa Masak My Style*. She was recently awarded a Lifetime Achievement Award for service to the transgender community.

....

To my trans sisters,

What you see before you is a transgender woman imbued with strength and perseverance to stand the test of time, and the multitude of challenges throughout my long career.

Yes, I have come a very long way to be here, and to be who I am today, but I would not change a single moment because it made me who I am.

My mom passed away when I was only five years old, and I have three older sisters, who all got married one after another and went to live with their husbands in Malaysia. I stayed with one of them while my dad went to Malaysia to search for a new wife, but after a couple of years, things didn't work out and I eventually came back to Singapore, to continue my studies here, but dropped out of school when I was 14 years old.

In my teens, I began to transition as back then we could purchase hormone pills easily over the counter without a prescription. The aim was to naturally develop breasts so as to have a better foundation for breast implants and also to feminize one's looks and skin – the result was fantastic!! I was overjoyed after a few days when my nipples started to swell like a virgin's.

I made friends for life with another transgender girl from my neighbourhood. Life was fantastic! We were young, so when we started getting attention from the boys...that's when our lives began. All this happened when I was living back at my dad's place, trying to hide it all from him. I had to keep my tiny purse of make-up and earrings away from his eyes, and had to wear a baggy blouse to cover up my cute tits.

I came back home one night, and my dad was waiting with my step-mom (he got married in Malaysia without my knowledge). They had discovered all my personal belongings. There was a huge row between my dad and I that turned into a fight. I left home and decided to live on my own.

I lived in the red-light district with some other transgender friends. There I started my life as a transgender woman at the age of 16. Life got better as I started to work on the street in the city, hooking up with Caucasian men and sailors. I made a lot of money and was too pretty to not discover relationships, and yes, I fell in love. Working on the streets, I met quite a few strange Caucasian men with all sorts of kinky fetishes that I didn't understand, but for money I'd do anything. My favorite customer was a French guy who lived just behind Orchard Tower, where many of us would hang out. He had an unusual fetish where he only wanted to pick up girls like us with red nails. We always had to have our finger nails painted and when I say 'we', he sometimes took three of us home. We were his favorites. All that he wanted us to do was tie him up and scratch him with our finger nails. I don't know how that could excite him, but who cares, we were happy to go with bucks in our Dior purses.

We would then run from Orchard Tower to Bugis Street, as many more foreigners went over there to enjoy the night till 6 am, all dressed up in our stilettos, purses and designer clothes – Ungaro, Arman Barsi, Montana – it was such a heavenly feeling. I had soon made enough to go for my first surgery, breast implants at the age of 17.

With all that I had, from breasts to Bugis Street, my life was getting there, so I went back to see my dad and his new wife, my step-mom. They were happy, but not that happy to see my condition. My step-mom had nothing much to say – give her a Coca Cola with a tiny bit of salt added and she's happy. My dad came up to me, looked at me properly and said, 'Whatever you do, you will not have my blessing until you're 21, when you are able to make your own decisions!' That was our last goodbye before his last breath.

My life started to change soon after, I was so obsessed with wanting to become a model – a female model! I went to one of Singapore's top modeling agencies and I took courses and modeling classes, and I learned how much social etiquette can change a person, taking them from zero to hero.

Around this time I was also hired to do a drag show in one of the clubs. We were only there for two months when the government introduced strict rules whereby we were not allowed to wear women's clothes unless we had undergone a sex change because in Singapore, after our surgery we are allowed to change our gender markers on our passport, etc. There was only a handful of us at the time and most of us had not had reassignment. The club was closed after a long battle with the government but I carried on modeling, doing photo shoots and runway shows.

Remembering what my late dad had said, at the age of 21, I went for my sex change in Bangkok with the famous Dr. Preecha. I did not have to go for a psychiatric assessment because I had had that done here in Singapore when I was assessed for enlistment in national service!! Every Singaporean male had to enlist to be in the army. I received my first appointment when I was 16, and it took me many appointments and attempts to be exempted from the national service. I wasn't enlisted because I went for my sex change at 21 and had my gender changed to female.

My life and career really began when I joined Singapore's only cabaret show, 'Boom Boom Room'. I became very popular, especially in the fashion industry. I worked hard to make a name for myself.

I chose this name when my school friend wanted to call herself Almi, and because we were so close I wanted to have a name that was not far from hers, so I chose Amy... Where did 'Tashiana' came from? Well, there was a very famous Russian model named Tatiana and I was dying to have this name on my ID card and passport but that wouldn't make me a Russian, I am still Malay, so I put the 'S' in the middle of Tatiana – the 'S' is for single, sexy, self-confidence and Singapore.

I retired from show business, modeling and ruling as 'The Queen' of the club scene in my thirties and began working as a choreographer, producing fashion shows across Singapore, China, Indonesia and Paris. I now have my own popular home cooking show Masak Apa Masak My Style where I teach the younger generations about the traditional Singaporean dishes created by our grandparents that have been lost over the years. I've also been working with the younger generation to preserve the tradition of transgender beauty pageants which have always been an important part of our culture and I recently set up an online support group for LGBTQ individuals in Singapore – Binary Singapore. I also still do talks and interviews to educate people about what it means to be transgender. The younger generation think of me as a pioneer – but it makes me feel old when I have to remember all the stories from back then!

I received a Lifetime Achievement Award from the transgender community here in 2017 and as the host of the show read out why I was receiving the award, I was amazed at my own achievements. How did I do it? A long struggle, understanding my surroundings and people, being humble, patient and polite – this is what many transgender people need to understand.

I believed in my dreams – make your dreams a reality too!

Beauty doesn't make a person, but beauty is what I have...not just what you see, but that elusive inner beauty that resides in my heart. I am not shy to share this, because my heart is an open book to everyone around me, sharing my love with those who need it and who mean so much to me.

I have worn many hats throughout my life and career, across fashion and entertainment, and now being a chef. Good and bad pass me by, but I let nothing stop me. Life has been my learning curve, and I'm still learning, adapting and living life to the fullest.

I dare to speak out loud that I LOVE MYSELF, and that gives me the courage to face this world and its challenges head on, every second of my life. My life story is still writing itself.

I invite you to join me, and continue my journey of life, for which I will fight fiercely till my last page.

Amy Tashiana

Martine Rose

....

Martine Rose is the founding and current Editor of *Repartee*, a magazine for the trans and cross-dressing community, which has been in print since 1989 and online since 2016. She has run the magazine single-handedly for the most part since its creation. She also set up 'Roses House' in 1979, as a place to provide comprehensive help and support facilities for the transgender community.

....

To my trans sisters,

I have been serving the trans community for 38 years, mostly from the perspective of considering myself to be transvestite rather than transsexual, though relatively recently I have transitioned fully to being female. Through all these years I have met, spoken to, and read the stories of many transsexuals in all stages of their journey from male to female (and a few the other way). The most common expression I hear is that they feel they are 'a female trapped in a male body' and they regard having the operation as correcting a mismatch between their brain and body at birth. I have tried to compare what they say with my own feelings about my gender and I cannot say I have felt the same.

From a very young age I have always had the wish that I had been born female and this wish only got stronger with time. But I have not felt this wish arose out of the way I was born; I just felt intensely jealous of females for their freedom to wear beautiful clothes, make-up, etc., and I thought that being a painfully shy person, life would have been so much easier for me if I were female in a world that still largely expected men to take the lead in those early days.

I reluctantly accepted that I had a male body, but who can say how a woman's brain works differently from that of a male? Physically there is very little difference between male and female brains, and mentally the differences are probably more nurture than nature. Analysing my own so-called masculine and female traits, I appeared to have a roughly equal mix of what most people regard as male and female. But I don't think that anyone having predominantly male or female traits necessarily makes them that gender. Not all men who are kind, empathetic and emotional (for example) feel they really should be female, and not all women who are good at map-reading and have an interest in technology want to be men.

I do wonder whether some of those who claimed the cliché, 'female trapped in a male body', were perhaps confusing that belief with an intense wish to be female. I thought maybe at least some of them were actually a bit more like myself but were perhaps less articulate in their thoughts to fully analyse the root of their feelings.

In *Repartee* Number 7, published in 1991, I wrote an article entitled 'Do you really want to change sex?', which was much acclaimed at the time and was also reproduced in a few other publications. I wrote it because I had been approached by many males who were clearly very confused about how they felt and were considering the route towards what was then commonly referred to as a 'sex-change'. There is less confusion these days because the public generally are much more aware of the whole trans situation but I still wonder whether for at least a few of those seeking gender reassignment surgery (GRS), it is a deep-seated wish to be of the opposite gender that lies at the root of this desire rather than any actual physical mismatch between brain and body.

I ask my trans sisters to question truthfully what you believe is the root of your desire to transition. If you are very honest and think that maybe it is a wish rather than anything physical, there is nothing wrong in that. You can still go ahead and transition (as I have done) as it can make your life just as unhappy if you continue to live in a gender that you feel is not right for you.

Also I can tell you it is never too late to transition. I had my op in March 2016, aged 76, and I do not believe I have been the oldest person to have done it. For most of my life I reluctantly accepted the fact that I had been born male and just cross-dressed when I could. The main reason for accepting the situation was that I felt heterosexually attracted towards women (not at all to males) and thought I'd have more chance as a male of finding a female partner. Partly because of my shyness, I did not have much success in forming relationships, but the hope was always there (and still is). However in my old age the realisation of that hope seems much less likely to be fulfilled and with a change in my circumstances it seemed I could at least realise my dream of living full-time as a woman. I had breast and facial feminisation surgery in 2007, and living successfully and happily as Martine since then has really helped my case when I applied for GRS.

I urge my trans sisters not to be too impatient in seeking the op. Live in the gender you wish to be (or believe you really are) for as long as possible before pressing for GRS. You have your whole life ahead of you. At 78 I believe I still have many years ahead of me living as the female I always dreamed that I could be.

Finally, please don't lose your femininity (if you are M>F) after you have had the op. I see so many who used to enjoy 'dressing up' as attractive women before but seem to lose interest after the op. I deplore seeing cis-women who just don't bother, and feel it's such a shame that some of our sisters feel that having changed there is no longer the need or desire to look good.

Whatever your dreams, I wish you all the best in fulfilling them.

With love,

Martine Rose

Missteary Manmade

....

Missteary Manmade is an American transgender rapper, activist and humanitarian. She began her music career in the all-trans rap group Pretty Thugz, eventually going solo, releasing her album 'The Rap Queen' which was featured on Worldstar Hip Hop garnering over a million views. She now splits her time between music and activism after recently co-founding the G.H.O.S.T. project, which sees her putting on events in the New York City area to support the trans and gender non-conforming community.

....

To my trans sisters,

When tasked with the job of sharing a few words of wisdom with my sisters of trans-experience from all around the world, I did not have to think long on it. It almost seems as if the words were already sitting on the tips of my fingers and ready to leap onto the page. Despite the many major issues currently plaguing our community, in my opinion, so much of our prosperity is centered on our self-value. Too often, we give others the power to diminish our self-worth and make us feel alienated and ashamed of our truths. I know sometimes the things we go through as transgender women can leave us feeling empty and unloved, but despite what lies you have been told and even the ones you may have told yourself, YOU ARE DESERVING! You deserve new beginnings and happy endings that are filled with better days and beautiful nights. You deserve basking sunshine in the morning and big, bright stars hovering in your darkness so you never lose your way. You deserve long hugs from loved ones that reassure your safety, and smiles that spread across your face from ear to ear. You deserve moments of victory and celebrations of success, voyages to conquer and mountains to stand on. You deserve love! And not just love, but an abundance of love. From somebody, to somebody, for somebody, and with somebody. You deserve to dream and to chase every dream you can dream until you're out of breath and your heart is racing so fast it feel like it's about to burst out of your chest. Your transition does not devalue you or reduce you to survival sex. Your transition does not limit your capabilities nor deplete your possibilities. Your transition is not your entire story. Life still owes you mystery and wonder, love and affection, exuberance and bliss, friendship and family, religion and faith, marriage and equality, babies and grandbabies. You are a butterfly erupting from its cocoon and leaping from the lip of a lily into a new, brave, stronger existence. And you deserve to be proud of that.

Yours truly,

Manmade!

Rachael Booth

....

Rachael Booth is a Vietnam navy veteran, linguist and author. She joined the US Navy during the Vietnam War, where she became a Mandarin Chinese and Arabic linguist. After a nine-year naval career and after transitioning in 1991, she went on to author her memoir, *Wishing on a Star – My Journey across the Gender Divide*, and more recently *The Port in the Cornfield*.

....

Dear sis,

It's me, Rachael – your future self. You did it! You made the change! It took you 40 years and lots of heartache to get there but it was all worth it. You did your best to try to fit into society as was expected of you – joining the Navy (a great decision, by the way), getting married, becoming a father. Those last two weren't such wonderful ideas. I know you were trying everything you could to find a way to be happy as a man because everything else just seemed so, well, so fucking impossible. It was the '70s and '80s for Christ's sake. But I just want you to know that being a husband and father comes with baggage that you're going to carry with you for a very long time. Keep in mind that every life you bring into your world as Ricky, whether a wife or a child, is one that you're going to hurt very badly later when you finally decide that you have to move forward. Don't get me wrong, it's great to have kids. They're going to give you beautiful grandchildren that you're going to be incredibly proud of. But your exes are going to be total stone-cold bitches and are going to do their best to keep the children from you as they're growing. You can't really blame them, though. They're hurt by either the realization of who the *real* person is they married or that they can't 'fix' you. You hurt them badly and they're going to respond in kind several times over. Stay strong, though. You can survive it. And you will have your children back in your life again.

You're going to survive so much. Living as a man is going to be hard. There's not going to be a day that goes by that you're not going to wish that you could find a way for something deadly to happen to you and make it look like an accident. You're not going to be able imagine that you're ever going to find the courage to go through with the change. But that's the key. You're going to come to the realization that you don't have to have courage to move forward and get your life right. You're going to discover that it's not courage at all – but conviction that if you don't try to fix your life, one day you're not going to be able to stop yourself and you're going to succeed in ending it all, vanishing from the earth without fulfilling your life and finally having the chance to be wonderfully, deliriously happy.

It's not going to be an easy thing to do, though – don't get me wrong. You're going to be faced with the derision of your peers at work and you're going to have to put up with silly rules about the bathroom enforced on you by the older women who can't and don't want to understand. They're going to make you carry around a big red sign whenever you want to go to the bathroom; and, after you knock on the door and make sure that no one's in there (or they finally leave and tell you the coast is clear), you'll go in, do your business and then take your sign back to your desk. You're going to feel like you're in kindergarten again – and it's going to suck. The older women at work are going to make you do this because they're going to be afraid that you're going to ogle them in there. (How? Stand on the toilet and peer at them from over the stall?) Or that you're going to physically assault them. (Not possible. You're going to be on hormones and couldn't get sexually excited if you wanted to.) Or, most ridiculous of all, that you'll leave AIDS on the toilet seat. (AIDS is a deadly sexually transmitted auto-immune disease that ran rampant through the gay community in the '80s and '90s. You have to laugh at this one. They think you must have been a gay man to want to do this.) But keep your sense of humor about this. It's only for a year – while you have to go through 'life test' living, working, and socializing as Rachael before having final gender confirmation surgery – that you'll have to put up with it. A lot of transgender people aren't even allowed to go to the bathroom inside the workplace. They have to go to a gas station down the road. You're lucky. Have fun with the sign. Talk to your Human Resources people and tell them you'll use the sign but you want some editorial fun with it. Make it say things like 'Come on in! The water's fine!' and 'I don't mind if you come in and pee with me!' Have a blast! And keep a running countdown at the bottom to remind people of how many days you're going to keep using this idiotic sign before you're anatomically correct. And you will be. Your body isn't going to be any different than that of any woman who has had a full hysterectomy.

Brace yourself for loss, though. You're going to lose friends who you didn't know were very religious and who seem to believe there's something in the Bible that says you can't change your gender (there isn't). They weren't your real friends, anyway. But the worst is going to be your parents. They're not going to embrace this at all and are not going to talk to you for almost 20 years. But don't give up hope. They'll come around and will eventually be comfortable calling you their daughter. This is going to be the hardest thing you're going to have to go through, but you can do it. It'll be all right in the end.

And you're not going to be a spinster in your new life, either. You're going to have some heartache just as you had as a guy. But you're going to finally find a woman who is going to be your soul mate and the two of you are going to grow old together. Really. Even this is possible. (By the way, don't date men. It will be a waste of your time and you're not going to like them very much.)

When you come to the realization that you have to go forward with your change or you're going to die at your own hands, the weight of the world is going to be lifted off your shoulders. It's going to be the most liberating thing you've ever felt and it's going to change your whole outlook on life. All those years of anguish are just going to melt away. Don't dwell on them, though. They're gone and there's nothing you can do about them. And when you do make your change, don't go back into another closet. Remember how horribly afraid you were that someone would find out about how you felt inside when you were trying to be male? You're going to find yourself back in that closet as Rachael, deathly afraid of someone finding out you used to be a man. You're going to waste a lot of energy trying to talk about your past life without lying. It's a great thing that you don't like to lie, but your brain is going to be so much on guard trying to come up with stories to cover your past without actually lying about it that it's going to drain you. People really aren't going to care when they find out about your past. You're wasting your time trying to hide it.

Embrace it. You are one of the strongest people anyone has ever met, having suffered through this hell all your life and come out alive and well on the other side. Tear down that closet and never go back into it.

You're going to finally be happy, Sis. I guarantee it. You're not even going to remember being Ricky. You're going to still have Ricky's memories, but somehow they're just not going to be tied to that male body. They're YOUR memories. You just had to live in the wrong shell while you were experiencing them.

One last thing, though: as soon as you make your decision to start changing, get to a laser electrologist as soon as you can and stick with them. Regular electrology hurts like hell and only gets worse the more female hormones you take. And your hair is going to turn white. Laser doesn't work on white hair. You're going to have to go through life worrying that your facial hair is showing. Trust me, that's NOT going to be fun.

Trust in yourself and in your inner strength. You have more of it than you know. And remember that little star you wished on, those warm summer nights when you sat outside as a five-year-old child, to make you a girl when you woke up? Well, first of all, that thing gleaming in the evening sky was probably Jupiter and not a star at all. It's OK. You were only five years old. But in any case, whatever it was, it's really, really far away. And if it helps you to think this way, it took 35 years for that wish to get there and come back to you to work its magic. But it did happen.

Stay strong, Sis. We will meet some day. And you're going to be beautiful.

I love you.

Rachael

Kuchenga

Kuchenga is a writer, activist and self-proclaimed 'agitator' from London. She is a member of Black Lives Matter UK, the Bent Bars Collective and Sisters Uncut. She speaks and writes on trans issues internationally, recently speaking about intersectionality at the Southbank Women of the World Festival. Kuchenga is also the Founder of Write or Die Publications.

....

To my trans sisters,

I am writing to you from my writing table in the living room of my one-bedroom home, the day after my eighth laser session. My skin is tender, the dog is comfortably curled up underneath the day bed and Japanese classical music is cleansing the space I inhabit. The peace and calm that I now surround myself with has been hard fought for. It's a gargantuan achievement.

The grand tragedy that was puberty became a war. A war against myself. There was something so deeply wrong with my existence, which I knew in my soul. That chasm grew larger and larger over the years. I used every drug in the world trying to fill it, to no avail. The men who beat and raped me made that hole even bigger. Each time my being was wronged in traumatic ways, the conversation with myself got deeper and more pained.

Transitioning was like the moon rising and pulling in the tide to wash a parched shore. Imagine a goddess with deep blue skin, braids flowing in a gentle night breeze in a coat of crystals beckoning you to the sacred. With her assistance, I begun to love myself in ways no one could have taught me how. Though the pain may not always feel worth it, as time marches on, the narrative makes more sense. The darkness of me being so rich, it can feed others endlessly.

This morning I chanted 'nyam myoho renge kyo' and I felt so whole and juicy. The 13-year-old me received guidance from Tina Turner that she could not have known would save her one day. The escape from an apartment that felt like a plantation into a land of freedom where my talent and intellect shone bright enough to have so many see me with love. The uniqueness of being trans is so precious. Our existence is dazzling.

The sisterhood I found online, in books and in real life, dispels on a daily basis the belief that we are all evil bitches. Far from it. I have met some wonderful bitches. Some who revel in sluttiness which waxes and wanes with one's whims or for business. Some who take one's breath away with wedding dresses and multifaceted careers. Some who illustrate the world in honesty through politics, art and technology. Sister TS Madison. Sister Janet Mock. Sister Kat Blaque. The blessings they've rained down on me can't be measured. With me at every appointment. Pushing me forward through every transphobic incident to make the tears nourishing. Helping me make the world see that all black lives matter.

Good, good girlfriends. My girl Natasha, who sponsored me into a still blossoming recovery and continually teaches me what compassion looks and feels like. My girl Eleyna, who made

South London a home of giggles and realness. My girl Frankie, who made a woman out of me on International Women's Day in an act of solidarity that won't be matched. My girl on the inside Kimberly, who taught me that a world without prisons is not an audacious thought. My sister Shupikai, who has made a sister out of me and loves me more than I ever thought possible. A deep radical African love forged in blood and literature that creates a world of possibilities that will also help free others.

Sisters! We are all we have got and that's more than fine because we are all we need. The fear and intimidation we inspire is because they know that the femme revolution has arrived. Standing on the backs of the bridges laid by sisters before us.

We rise.

We rise.

We rise.

Kuchenga

Gwen Fry

The Reverend Gwen Fry is an ordained Episcopal priest in the Diocese of Arkansas, with 26 years of service. She is the Vice President of National Affairs for Integrity USA, an LGBT organisation within the Episcopal Church, and a founding member of the Central Arkansas Integrity chapter. She is an advocate and activist for the transgender community.

To my trans sisters,

I'll never forget sitting in the living room of my grandmother's house as a teen. The whole family was there watching the US Open Tennis Tournament when a woman appeared on the screen and the commentators began describing the controversy surrounding Renée Richards.

It clicked for me in that moment. There was a name, an identity. And just as I was identifying with this new profound understanding of myself, in that truly sacred moment, I heard my family talking about her. My aunt said, 'He's a freak.' My dad said, 'He's a monster. He shouldn't be playing with the women, he's just a man dressed like a woman.' With that, a piece of me died. I buried that moment of self-understanding and discovery because I didn't want to be a freak...a monster.

I carried that with me for decades.

But after years of preparation and an extremely detailed transition plan, the day had finally arrived. February 19, 2014.

I was the Priest-in-Charge of a church in the Arkansas delta. It was a progressive parish for the town and I thought my chances for a good outcome were in my favor. That evening I came out to the Vestry (the governing board of the church). It was very well received, with the exception of one member. That person said to me, 'Well, are you going to preach from the pulpit this Sunday wearing eye shadow and have curlers in your hair?' And in that moment, I flashed back to my grandmother's living room. 'He's a freak... He's a monster.' By the end of the meeting we had mutually decided to embark on a period of education and conversation before any decisions were made.

On Sunday I would come out to the parish at large during a special coffee hour. (The Parish Hall was packed.) I had never before experienced the level of vulnerability I felt as I stood in front of the full Parish Hall coming out to them that I am transgender and answering questions afterward. Little did I know this was just the tip of the iceberg of the vulnerability that was yet to come.

On Monday the local delta newspaper was calling and Tuesday morning the story ran. front page. Top fold. Headline right under the papers banner...with photographs.

Late Tuesday morning the TV news media started asking for interviews, calling on my cell phone, and camping out in front of my house, hoping to catch me if I tried to leave. One news crew even knocked on my door with the camera rolling. But there were no interviews granted or statements made. You see, that was the plan in order to protect my family.

By Wednesday morning I saw what the outcome was going to be. After only a few hours of sleep since Sunday morning, trying to stay ahead of the curve with the people of the parish, it was clear that this wasn't going to end well. The parish was fracturing left and right and I couldn't bear to see this happen to the people and parish that I deeply loved...and still do.

So I called my bishop and told him that I wanted him to create a graceful way to bring the pastoral relationship to an end for everyone's sake but especially for the people of the parish.

Wednesday evening there was a special Vestry meeting in which the senior warden of the parish read a letter from the bishop that dissolved the pastoral relationship between me and the parish.

And just like that it was ended. There was a strange peace that fell over me as I excused myself and walked out of the building for the last time. Even as I grieved the loss of what could have been.

The Thursday morning after I lost my position in the church a friend called me and invited me to a very informal 6 pm service at parish on Sunday. She hadn't yet heard that I lost my job the night before but just wanted to offer a safe place, a sanctuary if you will, where I could just come and worship.

I wasn't sure if I would attend, but by the time Sunday evening rolled around, I realized that I needed to connect with God. So I got dressed for the service. It was the first time in my life that I left the house as Gwen and it was to attend church.

I wept as the Gospel appointed for that Sunday was read. It was the story of Christ on the mountain top physically transformed and what had been hidden was made known and seen by Peter,

James and John. For the first time I heard the words Christ tells the disciples after they have fallen on their faces out of fear: Jesus came and, touching them, said, 'Get up and do not be afraid.'

With all the chaos and turmoil of that week, I forgot it was the last Sunday in Epiphany, the Sunday of the Transfiguration.

It almost feels like a lifetime ago, those early days following my coming out and socially transitioning. I lost everything I had spent a lifetime building. I have come to know what it means to absolutely rely on the goodness and grace of others, because I didn't have the ability or resources to do it by myself. I have come to know and embrace my vulnerability. In many respects, it is a new life. A life I never expected that I would have. A life filled with an unending succession of transitions. A life in which I am gradually discovering that it is possible to love myself.

Gwen Fry

Kalki Subramaniam

....

Kalki Subramaniam is an activist, actor and the founder of the Sahodari Foundation, which works for the social, economic and political empowerment of the transgender community in India. She has also founded Sahaj International School, which is dedicated to serving transgender students who dropped out of the mainstream school system because they faced discrimination. She herself holds two Master's degrees. Kalki was the first transgender woman in India to star in a lead role in a motion picture, in the film *Narthagi*. On International Women's Day, Facebook chose Kalki as one of the 12 inspiring women of the world who use Facebook as a community development platform for empowerment, and she was named a 'Woman of Worth' by L'Oréal Paris. Kalki was recently invited to speak at Harvard University, where she received a standing ovation for her speech.

....

To my trans sisters,

Listen. It is amazing that you have this opportunity to read our letters. I write this to you from India, a land of diversity and rich cultural heritage. India is the spiritual capital of the world, true knowledge and wisdom have always been born here and have enlightened human kind for thousands of years. I believe I have a handful of drops. I give a drop of that knowledge from the ocean of wisdom.

You sure know the power of human thought. Our thoughts make up our actions and our actions make up our life. You are what you think. You are the sum of your thoughts. Your thoughts design your destiny. At this point of your life, you are here reading this because you DECIDED to read this. That decision is your thought.

We are trans and we are special. This road ahead of you will be filled with roses and thorns, sometimes with fewer roses and more thorns. If you step on the thorns and fall, remove them from your feet, stand up and keep walking. Life is a journey. When we stop, there is no meaning. Keep moving.

The first thing I want you to do is respect and love yourself. Nowhere in your journey should you self-pity, devalue, underestimate or hurt yourself. Stand tall. You are special, you are unique in the entire universe. Believe me, there is only one YOU. As a creation you are already complete. You strive to change your form through transition which is truly your own identity. Do it wisely. Plan your life ahead. There is no rush. Give enough time. That is very important.

Research and find the right information about your gender identity. There are many online tests on gender – go for them. Find an experienced and understanding doctor to help you. Know your body well. If you decide to take hormone therapy, try to go for natural supplements rather than synthetic ones.

Smile at people, make friends and help them. There are so many nice people out there who understand you, accept you as you are and will support you in your transition. My friends have been my biggest strength. During my transition and after, they took the responsibility of healing me. I owe a lifelong debt to them. I can never stand equal in their sacrifices and selfless love for me. I have an abundance of gratitude for them. Choose your friends and keep them forever.

Fall in love. If that love fails you, don't fall down. Don't lose heart. Keep going. It is so much more important to love yourself and move on. Let love find you. Don't be desperate.

Do remember that there is no complete man or complete woman in this world. If anyone ever existed as such, they could never understand the emotions of the opposite gender. In every man, there is a woman and in every woman there is a man. How much of a man is a woman, and how much of a woman is a man is what makes them. Makes us all.

Through these words, I give you more courage and love; I give you the strength to take wise decisions in your life. I wish you all good luck and success.

Lovingly,

Kalki Subramaniam

Lynn Conway

....

Lynn Conway is a computer science pioneer and innovator, and is considered to be one of the pre-eminent women in high tech today. As a young IBM researcher in the 1960s, Lynn made pioneering innovations in computer architecture but was fired from IBM after they found out she was trans. Lynn did not let this deter her and went on to invent scalable MOS (metal oxide semiconductor) design rules and simplified methods for silicon chip design. She was principal author of the groundbreaking Mead-Conway textbook *Introduction to VLSI Systems*, which had been used in over 100 universities by 1983, and she pioneered the teaching of these methods at MIT, launching a worldwide revolution in VLSI (very large-scale integration) microelectronic design in the late 1970s. Among her many major awards are the Computer Pioneer Award of the IEEE Computer Society, the James Clark Maxwell Medal of the IEEE and the Royal Society of Scotland, election to the National Academy of Engineering and three honorary doctorates. Lynn is listed in the Trans 100 List, and *TIME* magazine named her in 2014 as one of '21 Transgender People Who Influenced American Culture'.

....

Ever-becoming ourselves in an ever-changing world
In her moving poem 'The Summer Day', Mary Oliver poses the ultimate question: What do we plan to do with the one life we get

to live? Now in my 80th year I often reflect on her words...words that have helped me face head-on many challenges.

As we grow from observing and aspiring, to learning by doing, to exploring and adventuring, to earning our place in society, some steps along the way are very frightening. When taking such steps, I keep these words in mind:

'A ship in port is safe, but that's not what ships are built for.' – Grace Hopper

'You miss 100 percent of the shots you don't take.' – Wayne Gretzky

'Your time is limited, so don't waste it living someone else's life.' – Steve Jobs

'Play for more than you can afford to lose, and you will learn the game.' – Winston Churchill

We can also gain strength, hope and courage by seeking out and sharing the stories of others who've sailed high seas, especially stories about courage in the face of uncertainty such as this: *The Moth Presents All These Wonders: True Stories About Facing the Unknown* (Katherine Burns ed. 2017).

Great challenges and opportunities lie ahead, because of the ever-increasing rate of techno-social change now underway. We now experience ever-becoming ourselves surrounded by an ever-more-rapidly changing world!

As social philosopher Eric Hoffer reflects: 'In a world of change, the learners shall inherit the earth, while the learned shall find themselves perfectly suited for a world that no longer exists!'

So be careful! Don't just build 'expertise' and sit on it as time passes, for you'll surely be left behind. Jump out on the front of learning waves and keep on surfing...keeping in mind B. B. King's cool observation: 'The beautiful thing about learning is nobody can take it away from you!'

If you get stuck in a rut of familiar habits, rituals and thought-patterns, the words here will help you take back control over your life: *The Power of Habit: Why We Do What We Do in Life and Business* (Charles Duhigg 2014).

The bottom line: follow Bob Noyce's advice and 'Go off and do something wonderful.'

And have no fear: Embrace and enjoy the escalating rate of techno-social change, for it has a truly wonderful side effect – it's enabling us to live far further into the unfolding social-future than we could ever have imagined!

During treacherous passages, be very realistic, yet passionately persistent. As historian and activist Bertha Calloway reminds us: 'We cannot direct the wind, but we can adjust the sails.'

In extrema, as gonzo journalist Hunter S. Thompson coolly observes: 'When the going gets weird, the weird turn pro!' That can get pretty wild but some of us can get to love it. As Kurt Vonnegut says: 'I want to stay as close to the edge as I can without going over. Out on the edge you see all kinds of things you can't see from the center.'

Finally, what about love? For me, this little story speaks volumes: 'The Day I Became a Bird: A Tender Illustrated Parable of Falling in Love and Learning to Unmask Our True Selves' (commentary by Maria Popova www.brainpickings.org).

During your journey, think of the young ones all around the world who'll follow after us...eager to learn the ropes, navigate the seas of life and explore the future. What words will you leave to help them surf ever more wondrous waves of human exploration, innovation and experience? What words? As for me, I treasure sharing these words by the legendary French aviator and writer Antoine de Saint-Exupéry:

> 'If you want to build a ship, don't drum up people to collect wood and don't assign them tasks and work, but rather teach them to long for the endless immensity of the sea.'

Take heart, take care, be kind and have fun. I wish you all good fortune in the adventures ahead!

Lynn Conway

DivaD Magnifique

....

DivaD Magnifique is a member of The Royal Iconic Legendary House of Magnifique, and Mother of the House's European Chapter overseeing the UK, France and Sweden. DivaD has performed internationally at prestigious institutions such as the ICA in London and the Palais de Tokyo in Paris. DivaD has been featured in *Dazed and Confused* and *i-D* magazines and performed alongside Grammy Award-nominated singer FKA Twigs in her music video *Glass and Patron*.

....

To my trans sisters,

If only I knew back then what I know and feel now. Nevertheless, I do not regret or feel slighted in any way. Everything happens for a reason, in its time and in its place. But what I will say is that I am a late bloomer.

I come from a very strict, devout Christian family. I was in church at least 3–4 times a week. With my mother being head of the music and choir group, and my dad being the head of the technical team (lighting, sound and stage management), there was no getting away from going to church. You could even say all my siblings and I were born in the church. We all had a very sheltered upbringing.

My mother, being the disciplinarian, was all about 'the only places you need to be seen in is church and school' and with her being Sri Lankan it was also all about the image we kept up for the rest of the family and all the church folk. It pretty much was the case we were one way in front of people and another behind closed doors. Sounds quite clichéd, I know.

From as early as the age of five years old I could tell I was 'different'. I was already noticing that I was not doing all the same things as the other little boys, i.e. I would want to play with Barbie/ My Little Pony, I would want to dress up, or play hairdressers. My mum and my granddad (my mum's side) would always scold me for doing these things, so I was made to feel I was in the wrong and this only made me feel like there was something wrong with me. During my very early years I was not aware of what being gay was or identifying as another gender (from what I had been assigned), so as a child I was quite confused and made to feel I had to keep my feelings and behaviours a secret.

Fast forward to my adolescent years when I started high school: 'The emotional and tormented years!' This was when I had my first encounter of what bullying really was. I was teased for the way I looked, the way my voice sounded, how I walked, how I behaved, even to the point where things became physically violent. I got so depressed, so angry and bitter that I turned to alcohol, cigarettes, weed, I became bulimic and even attempted suicide. I always thought to myself that if only I was born a girl my life would be so much better, but I still was not aware of what being transgender was, what trans identity meant, or that people could transition. (Again, my childhood was very sheltered and I knew nothing about myself or the world.)

Being someone that always had a huge interest in dance, dance was my outlet, my escapism, my happy place, the way I could express myself without having to use words to even speak. I really wanted to go to college/university to study dance, or join a dance company/agency and make a living out of it. Sadly, my mum did not understand this (my dad always took my mum's side) and she always tried to tell me it was a hobby and nothing serious, I even danced in my church, but that is the only place my mother thought I should do my dancing. I soon discovered that my mother did not want me to dance professionally because the dance industry is filled with homosexuals and heathens and she did not want me to be surrounded or influenced by such people.

I lost my virginity when I was 21 to a person that was my first love and was my first of many things. It was during this time I felt like I had to finally admit to myself my sexual orientation and embrace who I was and not be afraid to accept it. All the flashbacks of my bullying and teasing were zooming past in my mind's eye. So standing in front of the mirror, looking at myself, I said, 'You are gay. I am gay.' I finally said it (out loud)! But it was not that easy – it was a stammer and a stutter to get it out; and even after I did say it, it still didn't feel 100 per cent correct, due to the fact that I never felt or saw myself as a gay man. I still struggled to put my finger on it! Bear in mind that my family knew nothing about what was going on or what I was doing.

2011 was the boiling point for me. I could no longer go on pretending and living a double life: one foot in the church, acting up for everyone, and the other foot walking through Soho going to all the gay bars and experiencing young gay life. I literally felt like I had a split personality trying to play all these different characters for different people. Enough was enough! One day I came downstairs to the living room where my mum was (just before that we'd had a heated argument) and I blurted out with such severity and conviction, 'I am leaving your church! I am gay! And I am in a relationship with a man!' My mother hit the roof, fell back to the floor and hit the roof a couple more times. She was so furious and my dad was just speechless. My parents had stopped talking to me for about two months or so while I was still living with them. Shortly after, I decided it was best for me to move out and have my own space.

I still dance and I am still very active in what I do. For those that do not know me I am DivaD Magnifique of the House of Magnifique (New York City). I am the European Mother of the House of Magnifique with Chapters here in London, France and Sweden, and a member of the ballroom scene community. The style of dance that I do is vogue and I have been voguing since 2010. Ballroom and voguing really helped me a lot on a personal level, a spiritual level and a mental level. It instilled a healthy confidence and appreciation for myself and the struggles/situations that I have experienced. It helped me to accept my family for how they are and how they think, even though they might not accept and understand me; and most importantly it finally flicked that switch at 27 years old and helped me realise and accept my identity as a transwoman. This part of my life I have not yet revealed to my family but only to close friends and loved ones whom I know give me their undeniable support and see me for the true woman that I am.

As I said previously, I am a late bloomer. I have yet to start any hormone therapy or any types of treatment and to an extent sometimes this made me feel less of a woman, or a fraud. But there was this one day I attended a panel talk at Goldsmiths University and I had the pleasure of talking to such a profound, beautiful, intelligent and successful transwoman. She told me (paraphrasing here) do not allow technicalities and other people's opinions determine and dictate your identity and your transition; your transition is your transition, your journey is your journey. These wise words were said to me by none other than the gorgeous Miss Charlie Craggs and it is these words that I carry with me daily. And it is these words that I give to all my trans sisters out there, no matter where you are in your journey. Remember your journey is your journey, your story is your own. I only hope that my endeavours, my achievements, my journey and my story provide a platform and opportunities for my sisters and my community to be inspired and lifted and to keep going strong.

All my love, hugs and kisses,

Mother DivaD Magnifique xox

Bamby Salcedo

....

Bamby Salcedo is the founder and President of the TransLatin@ Coalition, which advocates for the needs and issues of Trans Latin@ individuals residing in the USA. In 2015 she organised a demonstration disrupting the National LGBTQ Task Force's annual conference 'Creating Change', protesting the continuous transphobic murders in the USA. Her life story is depicted in the 2014 documentary *TransVisible: Bamby Salcedo's Story*, and she was also featured in the popular HBO documentary *The Trans List* in 2016. Bamby has spoken at the White House in 2015 about violence against trans women and in the same year was named one of *OUT Magazine*'s OUT 100 pioneers of the year. In 2016 Bamby also spoke at the United State of Women's Conference put together by the White House Office of Vice President Joe Biden, who Bamby shared a stage with during the opening plenary session.

....

To my trans sisters,

What I'd tell my younger self or any other person of trans experience is that it is important to understand the power that we have as individuals and as a community. When we learn to own our power we're able to create, design and architect our own destinies, which in turn will support us to exist in a marginalized society.

Bamby Salcedo

Charlie Craggs

....

Charlie Craggs is an award-winning trans activist...and now author, apparently. She is the founder of Nail Transphobia and has been travelling all over the UK nailing transphobia since 2013 and has just gone global, taking her campaign stateside in 2017. She uses the proceeds from her campaign to run free self-defence classes for trans and non-binary femmes. Charlie topped the *Observer's* New Radicals list of social innovators in Britain, was awarded a Marie Claire Future Shaper Award in 2017 and has been called one of the most influential and inspirational LGBTQ people in the UK by both *The Guardian* and the *Independent*. She has starred in campaigns for Selfridges, the Victoria and Albert Museum in London, and Stonewall, and has written and spoken about trans issues on the news (BBC, ITV and Sky), for numerous publications (*Vogue, Dazed and Confused* and *The Guardian*) and at the Houses of Parliament.

....

To my trans sisters,

So this is the last letter in the book. I mean naturally I was gonna leave myself to last and be the Beyoncé (even though I'm definitely a Michelle compared to all the incredible women in this book).

No, but seriously though, I wanted to be last so I could think very carefully about the message I leave you with as you finish this book. Initially, I thought practical transition tips would be most useful to you; like advice about presenting and passing as female – styling advice, make-up tips, how to cover a 5 o'clock shadow, etc. – the physical side of transition – but then I realized, as useful as they might be, this is what we get caught up in so often and what our entire transitions and lives often become centred around. When what really matters is what lies behind the clothes, behind the makeup...behind the 5 o'clock shadow (the struggle is real). So this is what I want to talk about and what I want you to take away from this book.

Now I'm pretty early on in transition, so I've still got a lot to learn myself. I *still* make massive fashion faux pas on the regular, *still* wear way too much make-up some days and look like a RuPaul's Drag Race contestant popping down the corner shop, and I *still* have to shave my damn face every morning even after over a year of laser – I told you, the struggle is real, sis. In fact, thinking about it, as I finish this book, I'm starting to wonder why I ever felt qualified to write it in the first place...but something I *have* learned in my few years since accepting myself as trans is the importance of just that: *accepting myself*.

I've known I was transgender since I was about four. It wasn't until I was 21 that I *accepted* I was transgender though. This is because I didn't want to *be* transgender. I didn't think life would be worth living with how hard it would inevitably be, but it got to the point where I was so unhappy living a lie and so dysphoric in my male body, that it wasn't worth living that way either. I truly hated myself. Then one summer night, as I stood in my bathroom contemplating suicide, I looked at myself in the mirror, staring into my eyes. They were sad, broken, dead...but they were also girl's eyes, and for the first time in my life I truly saw myself and I finally accepted myself as transgender.

As soon as I stopped fighting who I was and accepted myself, everything changed. Not physically – I had to wait almost two years to get onto hormones, thanks to our healthcare system here in the UK, but without even poppin' a single 'mone, without any surgery or laser, without even presenting as female, my perception of myself and my relationship with myself totally changed because I finally *accepted* myself. Accepting myself didn't mean I started to like the things I previously hated about myself but it meant I loved myself unconditionally, regardless of the things I didn't like. This both changed and saved my life.

Loving and accepting yourself doesn't mean you can't change the things you don't like about yourself. Surgery is a necessary part of many trans people's journeys to becoming comfortable in their body, my journey included. I've just had facial feminisation surgery (FFS) and though I'm happy with the results – it will help ease my dysphoria and make navigating the world a hell of a lot easier – I want to point out that all that's changed after FFS is my face. Nothing else has changed. I still make questionable sartorial choices, still wear way too much make-up, and still have to shave my damn face every day (TWICE SOMETIMES). My point is that after FFS you might love your face, but this doesn't mean you'll love *yourself* if you didn't already before surgery, and really that's much more important and should be your priority. Your beauty will fade (yes, girl, even after facial feminisation), but self-love and self-acceptance are forever. So don't just make things like laser hair-removal and saving for your surgery priorities; make loving and accepting yourself a priority. Make it your first priority, your main priority. There's no excuse; unlike hormones and surgery, there's no waiting list or price tag, so start today. Start now. Put this damn book down, look in the mirror and say, 'I love myself' and keep saying it every day until you start to mean it and believe it.

It is vital that we do love ourselves as trans women, because so many other people don't. In fact they *hate* us. Trans women, especially trans women of colour, are being slain. Literally. And when we're not being murdered, we are being assaulted verbally and physically in the streets, we are being mocked in the media, we are being rejected by our families and friends, we are being fired from our jobs, we are being put in men's prisons, we are having our education stolen from us, we are having our rights taken from us. You don't *need* to hate yourself; there are enough people doing that for you already, sis. In a world that hates us, learning to love yourself as a trans person is a revolutionary act.

When I began presenting as female, my life got so much harder in so many ways. The amount of transphobia I faced on a daily basis was debilitating and I was scared to leave the house most days. But although my life got so much harder, I was happier than I'd ever been because I was finally being true to myself and, more importantly, I finally loved and accepted myself. If you truly love and accept yourself, it doesn't matter what anyone else thinks about you, says about you, or does to you. If you've got yourself and I mean *truly* got yourself, that's all you need, sis. This is the most valuable lesson that I have learned and the lesson I want you to take away from this book.

So this book ends here, and your journey begins. It will be the journey of a lifetime, full of ups and downs. You will experience the lowest of lows but you will also experience happiness like you've never imagined, true happiness that only comes with living your truth. It will be a long journey, and there will be days when you feel a million miles from where and who you want to be, but on those days, remind yourself of the million miles you have already walked to be where and who you are now.

You're on your way and we're all right behind you.

I love you, sis,

Charlie xx